Early Roman Warfare

Early Roman Warfare

From the Regal Period to the First Punic War

Jeremy Armstrong

Pen & Sword
MILITARY

First published in Great Britain in 2016 by
Pen & Sword Military
an imprint of
Pen & Sword Books Ltd
47 Church Street
Barnsley
South Yorkshire
S70 2AS

ISBN 978 1 78159 254 0

A CIP catalogue record for this book is available from the British
Library

Typeset in Ehrhardt by
Mac Style Ltd, Bridlington, East Yorkshire
Printed and bound in the UK by CPI Group (UK) Ltd,
Croydon, CRO 4YY

Pen & Sword Books Ltd incorporates the imprints of Pen & Sword
Archaeology, Atlas, Aviation, Battleground, Discovery, Family
History, History, Maritime, Military, Naval, Politics, Railways, Select,
Transport, True Crime, and Fiction, Frontline Books, Leo Cooper,
Praetorian Press, Seaforth Publishing and Wharncliffe.

For a complete list of Pen & Sword titles please contact
PEN & SWORD BOOKS LIMITED
47 Church Street, Barnsley, South Yorkshire, S70 2AS, England
E-mail: enquiries@pen-and-sword.co.uk
Website: www.pen-and-sword.co.uk

Contents

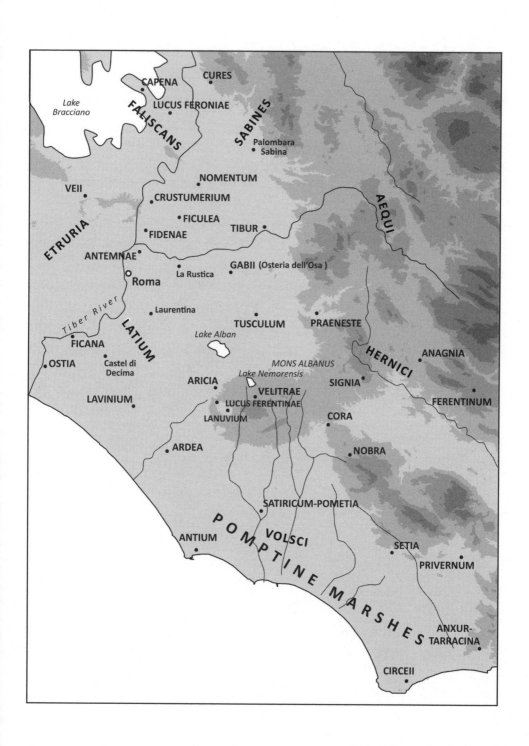

Introduction

The development of the early Roman army and the nature of early Roman warfare are complicated topics, and ones which have been the subject of sustained debate by historians in recent years. The very existence of this debate is perhaps a little surprising considering that the literary sources, superficially at least, seem to present a reasonably clear and coherent narrative for the evolution of Rome's armed forces during this period. Both Livy and Dionysius of Halicarnassus – our two main sources for the period – suggest that Rome's early tribal army, created by Romulus at the city's foundation in or around 753 BC, was transformed into something resembling a hoplite phalanx under the reign of Rome's sixth king Servius Tullius, as part of his 'Centuriate Reforms' sometime in the middle of the sixth century BC, and was then eventually 'broken up' into the famous 'manipular legion' in the late fourth century BC during Rome's wars with the Samnites. Each of these military changes coincided, at least roughly, with broad political and social developments within the city – including the foundation of the city, the aforementioned 'Centuriate Reforms' in the sixth century and the ending of the 'Struggle of the Orders' in the fourth century. The end result was the emergence in the early third century BC of a highly efficient military system which went on to drive Rome's territorial expansion during the next 200 years. The archaeology also, at least initially, seemed to support this model. Early excavations in Central Italy unearthed heavy bronze military equipment, most notably hoplons or *aspides* (the large circular bronze shields made famous by Greek hoplites), in contexts dating to the Archaic period – which seemed to corroborate the presence of hoplites and hoplite warfare in and around Rome during this period. And of course the existence and equipment of the later manipular legion is reasonably well attested by both contemporary literature and iconographic evidence. As a result, despite a few lingering questions and inconsistencies in the sources, this model has formed the traditional narrative for early Roman military and political development until very recently.

Scholarship in recent years has, however, increasingly called this narrative into question. There have always been issues surrounding the timing and nature of the various social and political changes in the narrative, and particularly the plausibility of massive changes like the 'Centuriate Reforms' occurring so quickly and at such an early date. Indeed, since the late nineteenth century scholars have 'tinkered' with this developmental sequence, arguing that the 'Centuriate Reforms' were introduced gradually or at a later date, while still trying to keep the overall model and linked military changes intact. Effectively, the explicit literary narrative preserved by Livy and Dionysius says one thing, but common sense (and a range of other pieces of evidence) point to something else. Consensus has yet to be reached on this matter, but it is noteworthy that the debate has been ongoing for over a century and the key questions have yet to be conclusively answered. More intriguingly, however, the military aspects of the traditional narrative have also been reinterpreted with significant repercussions. For instance, in recent years the biggest change has been the reassessment of the evidence for a Roman hoplite phalanx and its ultimate removal from the sequence of development by many historians. Traditionally, the presence of hoplite warfare and a phalanx in Rome represented the centrepiece of the narrative for the city's early military development, as it seemed to be well attested and provided a key point of comparison with the better documented Greek world of the fifth century BC. However, Roman historians only began to write down Roman history *c.* 200 BC, meaning that everything which came before that point was subject to problems of hindsight bias and increasingly fragmentary and problematic source material. Indeed, the historian Livy, in the opening of book six of his great history *Ab Urbe Condita* ('From the Foundation of the City'), famously noted that the events of the fifth century BC were 'like far off objects which are barely visible through the vastness of the distance'.[1] Despite this warning, many scholars have still been happy to take Livy and other historians at their word for the events of this time period. However, increasingly critical reinterpretations of the literary evidence, coupled with an ever-increasing body of archaeology material, has revealed that the presence of hoplites and hoplite warfare in Central Italy is likely to represent what might be called 'a historical mirage' (this particular issue will be discussed in detail later).

As historians have delved further into the nature of the historical tradition for early Rome, our understanding of how to read the extant material has developed substantially. When Rome's first historians sat down to write the history of their city, determining what early Rome looked like must have been like trying to decipher the picture on a 1,000-piece jigsaw puzzle based on only ten or fifteen pieces – an impossible task. As a result, it is clear that the early historians of Rome extrapolated and elaborated the limited evidence they had for the early city based both on their personal experience and understanding of Rome in addition to making things fit within their overarching story. This process of interpretation, elaboration and extrapolation continued with each subsequent historian who set about the task, with each writer changing or developing the narrative – although the exact amount of change between each version is unclear as only the last iterations, works by historians like Livy and Dionysius of Halicarnassus, actually survive today. All we know is that the historical record seems to have expanded dramatically with each new version, based on the fact that the earliest histories took up only a couple books (usually less than five to cover Roman history down to 200 BC) and the later books taking up many more (this same period took Livy thirty books). What this means for modern historians is that every scholar who attempts to tackle this period of history has, first of all, to decide how to deal with this problematic record, and there are no two approaches which are wholly alike – at least amongst those who specialize in the period.[2] Each approach, or methodology, for the sources is based on how reliable the scholar thinks this literary chain was – how accurately did the surviving work of a historian like Livy record the information which was passed on to him by earlier historians, and how accurately did those earlier historians report what they read in the histories written before them, etc? Each link in the chain is important, and there has been a tremendous amount of scholarship done on this 'literary chain' – although the final picture still remains frustratingly dark and confusing.

So, how have things developed? Although scholars still disagree (sometimes quite passionately) about many of the aspects of the narrative for early Rome, there has emerged a rough consensus on at least the problems with the sources, the nature of the sources for our sources (those cryptic accounts from the sixth, fifth and fourth centuries BC which later historians worked from) and what the writers of our surviving sources were trying to accomplish with their works (unfortunately, recording what we would consider 'accurate, factual, details' was not top on their list of priorities). This (admittedly limited) compromise has meant that many aspects of the surviving narrative can be effectively discarded, at least when attempting to determine what early Rome really looked like (they are naturally still useful in many other areas!), and has resulted in the emergence of a 'big picture' approach to early Rome. Increasingly, scholars have avoided focusing on individual passages or details in the narrative – at least in the first instance – as these could easily represent anachronistic insertions, and have instead attempted to see the 'big picture' behind the narrative – looking for broad trends and developments.[3] And, perhaps surprisingly (at least for some), the 'big picture' which many historians have found behind the scenes in the surviving historical narratives of early Rome bears only a passing resemblance to the explicit narrative presented in those same histories. In effect, there seems to exist a core disjunction between the underlying relationships, power dynamics and motivations present in the histories, and the overarching story which historians like

Livy were trying to tell. Something just doesn't quite fit. It is like setting a Shakespearean play in a modern setting (for instance Baz Luhrmann's movie *Romeo + Juliet* from 1996) – parts of it work, but certain parts stand out as being markedly anachronistic. Added to this development in historical studies has been the incredible advances in the field of archaeology. Once thought of as the 'handmaiden to history', useful only for illustrating or 'proving' various historical points, archaeology has emerged as a major force driving the reinterpretation of early Rome. From studying the physical remains of cities like Rome, Gabii, Ardea and Veii, to looking at funerary practices or determining the geography and landscape of Archaic Latium, the richness of Central Italy's archaeological record for this period has allowed interpretations of Archaic Roman and Latin society which can be viewed in isolation from the literary sources. Being able to compare and contrast the archaeological record with the underlying 'big picture' from the surviving literary accounts has breathed new life into early Roman studies, and a number of books and articles have been published in recent years which have endeavoured to weave these two strands of evidence into a single, coherent model. The resultant picture of early Rome has still varied quite widely depending on the specific methodology adopted, but a few broad principles have come through. Most notably, warfare during the earliest periods of Roman history has taken on a decidedly different flavour for many modern scholars, and indeed the entire sequence of Roman military development has been muddled quite a bit. The assumed state-based mentality behind much of the warfare practiced by Rome has increasingly been whittled away and a number of irregularities in the narrative, which had previously been consciously overlooked or argued to be 'errors', have begun to make a bit more sense – including the dominance of a raiding ethos in Rome's military activity during the fifth century BC and the ability of Rome's powerful families to engage in warfare, often on equal terms with the region's communities. Indeed, the fifth century BC is increasingly being seen as a period dominated by the region's powerful clans or *gentes*, which were only gradually incorporated into communities like Rome during the course of the century.

All of this has naturally caused serious issues for the traditional model of Roman military and political development, and at the present time there is not a single model or narrative which has gained consensus. A few basic points are increasingly accepted though. First, that Roman warfare during the early Republic was largely centred on raiding for portable wealth, and only gradually transitioned toward a focus on land in the later decades of the fifth century BC. Second, that there were likely a range of military models present in Central Italy – and in communities like Rome – which existed side by side (and perhaps overlapped) during this period. This range would have naturally included state-based armies, led by consuls (or similar leaders) and engaging in community-centred warfare. However, at the other end of the spectrum it also seems to have included clan and family-based military units, and most likely everything in between. There was no state monopoly on warfare in early Rome, and indeed the basic command structure seems to have relied more on existing clan power dynamics than state structures. Even in state-based armies, the *imperium*, or military command, wielded by generals in the field seems to have been drawn directly from the power of the *paterfamilias*, or head of family, and the goals were largely driven by personal ambition and motivation. Finally, third, that the emergence of the civic militia, which formed the core of the later Roman army, was in fact the product of a very long and convoluted series of political 'experiments', which included quite a few failures, and possibly only came to fruition in the fourth century BC. These 'experiments' included the creation of different magistracies, including the original consuls/*praetors*, the consular tribunes and finally the reintroduction of the consulship in 376/367 BC, along with various measures to delineate and ultimately expand Rome's available manpower. The final picture of Rome's early army which is therefore emerging in modern scholarship is vastly different from the traditional narrative.

Quick, massive changes followed by long periods of stability have been replaced by a long, slow and often painful development; and the Roman army, which was once thought to have had its origins in deep antiquity, is increasingly being pushed further and further forward in time, with the real origins of Rome's classic Republican army now appearing to be in the early fourth century BC.

This book will attempt to lay out and explain this revised model for the development of Rome's earliest armies and the interpretations of the literature, along with the advances in archaeology, which underpin it. As a result, although obviously relying heavily on the literary sources for early Rome – such as Livy, Dionysius of Halicarnassus and Plutarch – it will actually be arguing against their explicit narrative in many respects. It should therefore be noted at the outset that, although the broad picture presented reflects the general trends in modern scholarship, the specific narrative of development offered in this book is perhaps a little controversial and the ideas which are presented here are naturally not universally accepted. This is not because of a fault or issue in the argument or the approach (or at least the author sincerely hopes not!), but rather because there is not a universally agreed upon method for dealing with the problematic sources for this particular period of history. As a result, this volume is not attempting to establish the definitive 'correct' answers to the questions 'How did Rome's early armies develop?' and 'How and why did they fight?', as this sort of certainty is impossible for this period. Instead, it is simply endeavouring to present one *possible* model for development which takes into account the available evidence, along with the myriad issues and problems involved. The best way to read this book then (which is reflected in the way it is written) is to look at the big picture and not get caught up in the details.

Finally, a quick word about the intended readership. There is, honestly, not a single group this book is intended for, although if forced to name one it would probably be the 'educated enthusiast'. There is a general expectation that the reader will be roughly familiar with the grand scope of Roman history and will have a passing knowledge of the main figures and authors involved (Livy, Dionysius of Halicarnassus, Cicero, etc.), although it is hoped that just about anyone who sits down with this book will be able to get something out of it. As a result, a conscious effort has been made to focus on the 'big picture' (which also keeps the book in line with the scholarly trend in this regard), and only introduce specific literary passages, etc. when they might be particularly illuminating. Endnotes and references have also been kept to an absolute minimum (although obviously the narrative and argument contained in this book is based on the work of countless scholars!). If the reader is looking for a more 'scholarly' version of this narrative, there are any number of recent volumes which would be appropriate (see the back of the book for 'Further Reading'). Or, indeed, one can pick up the more academic (and footnote laden) volume on the subject by the same author (*War and Society in Early Rome* published by Cambridge University Press). But this book is meant to be a reasonably 'quick read', laying out the core arguments and narrative for understanding some of the modern views on the development of Rome's earliest armies and the nature of early Roman warfare, and hopefully encouraging further study into and interest in this exciting and dynamic topic.

Chapter 1

Rome's Regal Armies

T he study of the Roman army during the Regal period is largely an exercise in frustration. This is not because of a lack of evidence or ancient literature on the subject, as is the case with the Greek 'Dark Ages', as we have a number of detailed explanations of Rome's early military development preserved in the works of Livy, Dionysius of Halicarnassus, Plutarch and others. Nor is this frustration due to conflicts between these sources; indeed far from it as they are all generally in agreement on almost all of the major points. The primary issue which one faces when looking at the Roman army during this early period is that the ancient authors, who worked so laboriously to explain the structure of the early army, most likely had very little idea what they were talking about. This all relates back to the nature of Rome's historical tradition.

Rome was traditionally thought to have been founded in the middle of the eighth century BC and seems to have grown gradually during its early years until, benefiting from its key location on the major trade routes running through Central Italy (and particularly those between Etruria in the north and the Greek colonies in Magna Graecia in the south), it blossomed in the late seventh and sixth centuries BC into a major trading hub and urban centre. Despite its burgeoning wealth and population, the city seems to have maintained a local focus and outlook and it was not until the middle of the fourth century BC that the city had come to dominate all of Central Italy. From this point on, however, a 'critical mass' seems to have been reached and Rome's expansion picked up speed rapidly. By the early third century BC the city had defeated the army of Pyrrhus, showing that it was a major player in Mediterranean politics and

warfare, and controlled almost the entire Italian peninsula. By the end of
the third century BC Rome had defeated her greatest rival, Carthage, in
the Second Punic War and found herself as the only real power left in the
western Mediterranean. It was only at this point that the Romans decided
to sit down and write the history of their city – more than 500 years after
Rome's traditional founding and after the city had become one of the
most dominant powers in the known world – and this very late start for
Roman historiography created quite a few problems.

The first Roman historians seem to have been driven by a desire, very
similar to that expressed by the great Greek historian Polybius a generation
or two later, to explain Rome's rise to power – both to themselves and to
their new subjects. As a result, when they looked back on the history of
their city they did so with a reasonable amount of hindsight bias. They
knew how the story ended, they knew what Rome would become, but
they wanted to explain the journey – the keys to the city's success. The
main problem which these historians seem to have faced, however, is that
the information and evidence with which they had to work was wholly
inadequate for the task. The most important sources available to these
first historians seem to have been a series of annalistic accounts, the most
famous of which was that kept by the *Pontifex Maximums* or chief priest
in Rome, which recorded important events in the life of the city each
year. These *annales* were composed of entries which were initially written
on tablets posted outside the house of the *pontifex* and, in the case of the
records kept by the *pontifex maximus*, were later stored and traditionally
compiled into a single volume by P. Mucius Scaevola in the late second
century BC. However, the information which was contained in the *Annales
Maximi* (as these particular records were known), and the other yearly
records (for instance those kept by other priesthoods and sources like the
consular and triumphal *fasti*) was not written down with a grand history
in mind. Leaving aside basic issues of accuracy (and scholars still debate
these rigorously), these annalistic sources would have provided at best a
basic skeleton of events – including who held office, eclipses, famines,

wars, etc. – but would not have included any narrative elements or the structural details of Rome's early development. The bulk of this material must have come from Rome's enigmatic and problematic oral tradition.

Rome's oral tradition can best be described as 'multifaceted'. Cato, writing in the second century BC, said that some aspects of early Roman history had been preserved in songs sung at banquets, although these seem to have fallen out of fashion by the late Republic. We also know that there were plays being performed from at least the fourth century BC which were set in early Rome, called *fabulae*, and likely focused on early Roman myths. Additionally, there were the oft-maligned family histories (which Cicero and other writers claimed were largely fabricated), which became most strongly associated with Roman funerary orations, where the deeds of ancestors were recalled each time a member of the family passed away. And there were likely a range of stories and myths which had been passed down through the generations through simple storytelling and 'collective memory'. The reliability of this oral information, however, is highly suspect. As modern research on oral traditions has shown, while a surprising amount of information *can* be transmitted through the generations, it is usually adapted for each audience. As a result, while certain overarching themes and narratives from Rome's early history were likely preserved, the oral tradition is not the best mechanism for preserving the detailed structural information which historians of early Rome (and particularly the early Roman army) crave. So when Rome's first historians sat down to write histories of their city, working in a genre which had, by that point, a very long history in the Greek-speaking world with well-established rules, they were decidedly ill-equipped in terms of evidence. Rome's first native historian, the aristocrat Fabius Pictor writing *c.* 200 BC, is likely to have had access to his own family history and those of a few other families, probably knew the main myths/stories about Rome's early history (Romulus, Remus and the she-wolf, the Battle of the Champions, Brutus and Tarquin, etc.), and may have been able to go through some of the priestly records. But it is also likely he had to flesh the narrative out quite a bit using some common-sense and his own understanding of Roman society – and even so, his history of the early periods seems to have been rather short. Unfortunately Fabius Pictor's history does not survive today, nor do the attempts of his contemporaries, although we can say that they all seemed to have been brief accounts. Cato the Elder's history of Rome, for instance, consisted of seven books in total with the first three devoted to the origins and early history of Rome and the cities of Italy.

Once Fabius Pictor wrote his history, however, historical writing picked up very quickly in Rome and he was followed by a line of other writers who all wanted to add their own spin to the story. During the course of the second century BC, historical writing flourished in Rome and a number of new histories were written by authors who are now known as the *Latin annalists*, because of their progression through Roman history in a year-by-year fashion. Perhaps surprisingly though, despite the fact that these historians did not seem to have access to any more original evidence from early Rome than Fabius Pictor or the other early writers did, these new histories often included much more material for the earlier periods than those written before.[1] The historian Cn. Gellius for instance, writing in the second half of the second century BC, did not reach the year 386 BC until book fifteen of his history, and he did not get to the year 216 BC until either book thirty or thirty-three. Although Cn. Gellius likely represents an extreme example, it has been argued that there was an overall 'expansion' in the history of early Rome during this period as each writer added his own details and explanations to the cryptic core of evidence. Indeed, it is likely that historians stopped consulting the original evidence altogether and often worked simply from the works of previous historians, adding their own extrapolations and interpretations to the inventions of those who came before.

The annalistic tradition came to an end in the late first century BC with Livy and his great work *Ab Urbe Condita* ('From the Foundation of the City'), a 142-volume history of Rome from its earliest days down to the reign of Augustus – of which the first ten books are devoted to Rome's history up to the year 292 BC.[2] Livy's work was so successful, and accomplished its goals so conclusively, that he effectively ended the annalistic movement and the creation of grand histories of Rome – although part of this may have also related to the change in political climate under Augustus and the later emperors. Writers like Tacitus continued to write histories under the Empire, but no one attempted the same all-encompassing history of Rome that Livy had written and indeed his work was so popular that it supplanted, and resulted in the loss of, those histories which came before. However, Livy's account of early Rome, despite its success and the ten books he devoted to the subject, was still limited by the nature of the evidence which had been transmitted to the late Republic from the Archaic period – the authentic material in his history could not exceed that which was passed down from the Archaic period. As a result, although obviously engaging, well-written and very likely well-researched, there seems to have been no way for Livy to have known for sure many of the details he included. Unless there existed another resource or depository of information available to Livy or his predecessors which we know nothing about, much of Livy's history must represent an historical invention/elaboration on his part, or on the part of one of his predecessors, which would place it's origin at the earliest in the late third century BC. This is not to say that Livy, Fabius Pictor or the later Latin annalists were being deceitful and 'fabricating history' – something which a modern historian would likely be accused of if they tried something similar. Rather, it must be understood that 'history', as it existed in antiquity, was not so much about the 'facts' as it was about 'teaching a lesson'. Recording true details, although seen as important, came second to the pedagogical and rhetorical aim of a work. As a result, while ancient historians clearly attempted to record, as accurately as possible, events from the past if they were known, where there were gaps or *lacuna* in the evidence, or where the evidence was mythic or a bit malleable, they had no qualms about adding to the narrative to make their point. This is a practice perhaps best seen in historical speeches which, apart from a few exceptions where we know they were written down and preserved, often represented an opportunity for the historian to present what he felt would have been said in a given situation.

When one looks at the history of early Rome then, if the reader will forgive an indulgent analogy, the situation resembles interpreting the night sky. Looking up on a clear night we are confronted with a few bright stars, which we can understand as the evidence from the *annales* and perhaps aspects of the oral tradition which were likely transmitted, one way or another, from the Archaic period. These bold, bright structural points have then been interpreted by ancient writers into constellations, or the sweeping and detailed narratives presented in their histories. Often these histories have but a passing relationship to the evidence, just as constellations often do to their constituent stars, but they link them together in a fashion which makes sense to the observer and helps to give order to the cosmos. However, different people looking at a collection of stars will often come up with different constellations – and the same is true with early Rome. As modern historians, we must see through the preconstructed constellations, the detailed narratives presented by Livy and others based on their view of how events occurred, and go back to the basic evidence which was likely transmitted and analyse it ourselves. We must identify the key bits of evidence used by the ancient authors in constructing their narratives, look a bit more closely and perhaps identify some other structural aspects which they included in the narrative but did not recognize the importance of, and ultimately construct our own interpretation based on our modern understanding of how societies work and develop. This is, perhaps, one of the great advantages which modern historians have over their ancient counterparts. Although Livy and Fabius Pictor may have had a better understanding of their own culture as it existed in the late Republic, they lacked the myriad comparative societies which we have at our disposal today to help fill in the gaps in the evidence.

But first, we must begin with what the Romans thought things looked like in the Regal period.

The Traditional Model

The traditional model of Roman military development (which can be found in the 'standard textbooks' on Roman history, available in most bookstores) is largely based on a few asides within the larger narratives of our surviving sources, where the author stops his story to explain a detailed structure or development. It begins, of course, with Rome's founder – the quasi-mythical figure of Romulus – and his organization of Roman society into three tribes (the *Ramnes*, *Tities* and *Luceres*) and thirty *curiae*. The story goes, as relayed by Livy and Dionysius, that Romulus founded the city with a mixed group of followers which ranged from powerful clans to runaway slaves and asylum-seekers. In order to bring these disparate groups together into a single state and, perhaps more importantly, a single army, he created the two sets of divisions – the tribes and the *curiae* – which both seem to have had social, political, religious and military aspects. The relationship between the tribes and *curiae*, and indeed their fundamental character and make-up, are still a matter of some debate in modern scholarship (as will be discussed later). The ancient sources, however, are generally consistent on the matter, with Dionysius of Halicarnassus offering the most explicit account of their creation where he describes the *curiae* as mere subdivisions of the tribes, following the Greek model.

> He [Romulus] divided all the people into three groups, and set over each as leader its most distinguished man. Then he subdivided each of these three groups into ten others, and appointed as many of the bravest men to be the leaders of these also. The larger divisions he called tribes and the smaller *curiae*, as they are still termed even in our day.... These *curiae* were again divided by him into ten parts, each commanded by its own leader, who was called *decurio* in the native language.[3]

This system of tribes and *curiae* formed the basis for at least one political body, the curiate assembly, and offered a rough hierarchy for the army, although there are only vague hints given in either Livy or Dionysius regarding the details of the army during this period.

The standard size of the Roman legion (or levy, from whence the word is derived) during this period is often assumed to have been 3,000 infantry and 300 cavalry, based on both the structure of the tribes and *curiae* and assertions by both Livy and Dionysius about the initial contribution of each of the *curiae* (given as 100 infantry and ten cavalry). This figure is corroborated by the late Republican antiquarian Varro, who claimed that the early legion contained 3,000 men, with 1,000 coming from each tribe,[4] and the historian Plutarch, who gives the same number in his life of Romulus, although he adds 300 cavalry.[5] However, both Livy and Dionysius also seem to imply that this figure represented a minimum or a starting point, as opposed to a standard legion size, as Dionysius noted that when Romulus died Rome's forces far outnumbered this – although it is possible that the thousands mentioned by Dionysius merely reflected Rome's manpower reserves.

> By these and other like measures he [Romulus] made the colony great from a small beginning, as the actual results showed; for the number of those who joined with him in founding Rome did not amount to more than three thousand foot nor quite to three hundred horse, whereas he left behind him when he disappeared from among men forty-six thousand foot and about a thousand horse.[6]

As far as equipment and tactics are concerned, the literary sources offer us very little until the sixth century BC and the reforms of Rome's sixth king Servius Tullius. The battle descriptions from the life of Romulus and the other early *reges*, if they can be considered even remotely factual, suggest that both massed combat and duels were common and support the idea that Rome's army contained both infantry and cavalry. Unfortunately, military equipment finds from Rome itself are incredibly scarce for the Regal and early Republican periods, but what does exist for the eighth and seventh centuries BC – largely from graves in the *forum Romanum* – shows a mixture of swords and spears, along with a few pieces of bronze armour, which is generally supportive of this picture of mixed combat. This limited archaeological evidence is often bolstered with contemporary finds from elsewhere in Central Italy. Graves from other Latin sites dating to the eighth and seventh centuries BC have contained very similar finds to the graves in Rome, with swords, axes and spear points predominating, along with the occasional bronze helmet or breastplate. Graves from Etruria in the north, along with finds from Umbria and the Ager Faliscus, have contributed to the archaeological picture for this period as well with quite a few more helmets and elaborate circular shields – although whether these should be considered indicative of Roman equipment is still uncertain. Generally though, a very heroic and arguably Homeric style of combat comes through quite strongly in the available evidence.

After the army's creation in the eighth century BC, the traditional narrative holds that the sixth century BC was the next real period of change – a period which also coincides with significant growth and urbanization within the community and the emergence of the so-called 'Grand Rome of the Tarquins'. At the beginning of the sixth century BC, Rome's cavalry was expanded by the Roman *rex* Tarquinius Priscus (trad. *c.* 615–580 BC), but the most significant change occurred under Servius Tullius (trad. *c.* 580–530 BC) who transformed the army, and indeed all of Roman society, via a wide-ranging series of reforms often dubbed 'The Servian Constitution' or the 'Centuriate Reforms'. According to the narrative, Servius Tullius conducted Rome's first official census and reformed Rome's Archaic system of tribes by separating them from the *curiae* and basing them entirely on geography. These new tribes included four urban tribes and seventeen rural tribes – a number which was gradually expanded during the Republic to reach a total of thirty-one by 241 BC. This new tribal structure formed the basis of Rome's new Tribal Assembly, which represented Rome's burgeoning population and included both the urban inhabitants and an increasing number of powerful rural clans. Rome's army, however, was separated from this structure and was recruited instead from a new set of socio-economic divisions based on the census. The entirety of Rome's population was subdivided into seven socio-economic classes, each with a minimum level of wealth required for entry. At the top of this new system were the *equites*, which required 100,000 bronze asses (bronze coins weighing one Roman pound) along with a certain social position for entry, followed by the first class which required only the 100,000 asses, the second class 75,000 assess, etc. down though the fifth class and finally the *capite censi*, or 'head count' which was made up of the poor and did not contribute to the army. Each class was then further subdivided into centuries, with the *equites* containing eighteen, the first class eighty-two, the second class twenty, the third class twenty, the fourth class twenty, the fifth class thirty-two and the *capite censi* one.

The centuries of the Servian Constitution are incredibly problematic and have often been misinterpreted. One of the most glaring misunderstandings is that each century contained 100 men or was responsible for contributing 100 men to the army – neither of which seems to be the case. Dionysius in particular explicitly states that the centuries were merely administrative/recruiting units and did not contain 100 men each.

> For instance, whenever [Servius Tullius] had occasion to raise ten thousand men, or, if it should so happen, twenty thousand, he would divide that number among the hundred and ninety-three centuries and then order each century to furnish the number of men that fell to its share.[7]

Instead the name 'century' may have been derived from the number of divisions in the original census (the eighteen centuries of the *equites* plus the eighty-two of the first class together equalling 100), with the later classes/centuries being added later. Indeed, according to a passage attributed to Cato the Elder, as late as the second century BC the first class of the Servian system along with the *equites* were together known simply as the *classis*, with the lower classes carrying the designation *infra classem*.[8] The centuries themselves seem to have had no tactical function and were largely administrative in nature as they formed the basis for Rome's new Centuriate Assembly as well as representing the means by which Rome's army was levied. Each class was also associated with a particular military panoply or set of equipment, which members would have been expected to supply themselves as part of being in the civic militia. The *equites* naturally constituted the cavalry while the first class was equipped with a helmet, round shield, greaves, mail, sword and spear. The second class was equipped with a helmet, oblong shield, greaves, sword and spear. The third class was equipped with only a helmet, oblong shield, sword and spear. The fourth class, according to Livy, was composed of light infantry equipped with a spear and javelin, while Dionysius suggests that this group also carried oblong shields and swords. The fifth class carried nothing but missile weapons, and the *capite censi* did not contribute to the army at all, presumably as they did not have enough wealth to equip themselves with the appropriate weaponry.

The standard interpretation of the Servian Constitution is that it represented a shift from an old family-based, tribal system of government to a new state-centred democratic/oligarchic system similar to that present in Greece at this time. On the military side of things, this shift is typically seen to represent the transition from a highly individual, heroic style of warfare to something resembling a community-based hoplite phalanx. And indeed the Romans themselves seem to have thought that they once fought in a hoplite phalanx, a tactic which they claimed that they acquired from the Etruscans at some point during the Archaic period. Although this can be seen in both Livy and Dionysius' account, the best evidence can be found in the so-called *Ineditum Vaticanum*, which purports to give a speech by a Roman named Caeso (probably Caeso Fabius) to a Carthaginian envoy before the First Punic War, detailing Roman military development to that point and showing why they would be victorious in a war despite being woefully inexperienced at naval combat.

This is what we Romans are like ... with those who make war on us we agree to fight on their terms, and when it comes to foreign practices we surpass those who have long used them. For the Tyrrhenians used to make war on us with bronze shields and fighting in phalanx formation, not in maniples; and we, changing our armament and replacing it with theirs, organized our forces against them, and contending thus against men who had long been accustomed to phalanx battles we were victorious. Similarly, the Samnite shield was not part of our national equipment, nor did we have javelins, but fought with round shields and spears; nor were we strong in cavalry, but all or nearly all of Rome's strength lay in infantry. But when we found ourselves at war with the Samnites we armed ourselves with their oblong shields and javelins, and fought against them on horseback, and by copying foreign arms we became masters of those who thought so highly of themselves. Nor were we familiar, Carthaginians, with the art of siege craft; but we learned from the Greeks who were highly experienced in the field, and proved superior in siege craft to that accomplished race, and indeed to all mankind. Do not force the Romans to engage in affairs of the sea; for if we have need of naval forces we shall, in short time, equip more and better ships than you, and shall prove more effective in naval battles than people who have long practised seafaring.[9]

More importantly than the question of whether or not the Servian reforms ushered in an era of hoplite warfare in Rome, the new constitution very clearly represented the shift to an entirely state-centred military force. While the previous tribal army seems to have been controlled by the state and was led by the Roman *rex*, the basic units and recruitment of the army were still based on a series of pre-existing family and clan-based connections, which presumably gave those entities a fair amount of power. The new Servian tribes and system of classes broke down these old connections and created new ones dictated entirely by the relationship to the community. According to the literary narrative then, the army which emerged from the Regal period was very different from the one created by Romulus. The army of Servius Tullius arguably represented the first truly 'Roman' army and could be viewed as the ancestor of Rome's late Republican legions.

Criticisms

Although a neat, tidy and internally consistent model, this traditional account, based on the explicit testimony of our two main literary sources, has always faced a bit of criticism – and particularly the Servian reforms of the mid-sixth century BC. From a very early date scholars have wondered whether a system as complex as the Servian Constitution could have been introduced in Rome in the sixth century BC. It was suggested that the political aspects of the reforms, and specifically the creation of two new assemblies, made no sense in a Rome which was still ruled by a *rex*. Indeed, neither of the Servian Constitution's two new assemblies, the Tribal Assembly and the Centuriate Assembly, are recorded as performing *any* functions or duties until at least the fifth century BC. All of Rome's political power seems to have remained with the *rex*, the senate and the old curiate assembly which continued to pass the law granting/confirming *imperium*. Additionally, questions have been raised about whether Rome would have needed (or even would have been able to field) the elaborate military system laid out in the reforms during this period, with the wide variety of troop types described (including engineers and trumpeters). One possible solution to this issue is that the Servian Constitution, as preserved in the accounts of Livy and Dionysius, represents the final version of something which was only started in the sixth century BC. As noted above, given the passages from Cato, Festus and others, it seems likely that only the first class and *equites* were really thought of as the *classis*.

Not all of those in the five classes are called the *classici*, but only the
men of the first class whose census rating was 125,000 asses or more.
Those who are called *infra classem* are the men who belonged to the
second class as well as all the other classes, whose census ratings
were below that of the first.[10]

The term *infra classem* refers to those whose census rating is less
than 120,000 asses.[11]

These references, and others like them, have suggested to scholars that
the Servian system of classes actually developed slowly over time, with
the first class and *equites* being introduced first, and the later classes
being slowly introduced at later dates – possibly as late as the fourth or
third centuries BC. So the Servian constitution of the sixth century BC
may have simply been a rationalization and reorganization of the existing
tribal army based on economic and geographic criteria.

This still does not, however, explain the entire situation. Perhaps the
most damning criticism of the Servian Constitution and the traditional
model of Roman military development has come from increasingly
careful analyses of the literary narrative itself. Outside of a few 'structural
passages' in the literary tradition (essentially where the narrative stops
and a bit of detailed information is given by the author on various aspects
of early Roman military and political development), the literary narrative
for early Rome seems to describe the Romans fighting wars and engaging
in battles using a system which does not align with the precepts of the
Servian model at all. Instead of fighting wars over land and control of
territory, which would suit a community-based hoplite phalanx, during
the late sixth and fifth centuries BC the Romans and their opponents seem
to engage almost entirely in raiding for individual glory and wealth – a
style of warfare for which a phalanx is decidedly ill-suited. Additionally,
the few direct references to the Romans using a phalanx in an actual
battle situation are surprisingly problematic. For instance, Dionysius of

Halicarnassus describes the Roman army fighting against the Sabines in a phalanx.

> For their foes, despising them because their troops were new recruits, encamped over against them, and placing ambushes on the roads, cut off the provisions that were being brought to them and attacked them when they went out for forage; and whenever cavalry clashed with cavalry, infantry with infantry, and phalanx against phalanx, the Sabines always came off superior to the Romans, not a few of whom voluntarily played the coward in their encounters and not only disobeyed their officers but refused to come to grips with the foe.[12]

However, he also describes the tribal Sabine people as fighting in a phalanx and the entire passage is placed in a context of irregular warfare. As a result, it could be argued that Dionysius is using the word 'phalanx' to simply mean a group of infantry. This type of interpretation is supported by passages like this one, from a later battle narrative.

> Against the troops who were fighting in the middle of the phalanx, which was widely spaced and lax, those who were stationed here charged in a body and drove them from their position.[13]

Additionally, as noted above, although Roman society was supposedly reformed with military and political power being handed to the Centuriate and Tribal assemblies, neither of these assemblies seems to be active until the middle of the fifth century BC at the earliest. Instead, Rome's military and political systems seem to be dominated by a collection of powerful clans and individuals who seem to have had a fairly limited connection to the community. During the Regal period, the city of Rome and her citizen population often seems like more of a bystander than a major player in much of the warfare taking place. So, where did this standard model come from? Why did the Romans think they fought in a hoplite phalanx, if they did not? The answer may lie in the historical tradition itself. Intriguingly, the Roman army which the literary sources describe emerging from the Regal period mirrors, almost exactly, the military situation which Greek and Roman historians seem to have envisioned for Greece at the end of the sixth century BC – and particularly the emergence of the classic hoplite phalanx and the reforms of Cleisthenes in Athens. Whether the ancient Greeks were correct in their view of their own history, and particularly their military development, is still quite a contentious issue in modern scholarship – with scholars like Han van Wees challenging the traditional models and suggesting that the classic hoplite phalanx and hoplite warfare which the sources seem to describe may have represented an idealized version of what was fundamentally a more often individual style of combat. However, the emergence of heavily armoured infantry in the sixth century BC, coupled with social and political reforms, would have made sense to someone familiar with this model. And when the Greeks started to write their histories of the Romans in the third century BC (it should be remembered that the first histories to mention Rome and discuss her origins were written by Greeks), after Rome's emergence onto the Mediterranean stage with the war against Pyrrhus, and when the Romans settled down to write their own histories a couple generations later at the turn of the second century BC, they naturally looked at the strong historical precedent set in Greece and may have, either consciously or unconsciously, modelled their own narratives upon it.

Revised Literary Approach

Unfortunately, when it comes to looking outside the passages that form the basis for the traditional interpretation of the early Roman army, there is little solid evidence with which to work to create an alternative model. As a result, any attempts to assign concrete numbers, divisions or attributes to the early army will always represent guesswork (although perhaps educated guesswork) at best. The ideal complement of 3,300 men which the literary sources give for the *curiate* army of Romulus undoubtedly represents a rough estimate, based on what must have been a very muddled tradition, and it is clear that Romans did not envisage Rome's later Regal army, as organized by the Servian Constitution, as ever having a set size. So it is probably best to consider Rome's armed forces during this period as being flexible and reactionary, mobilized based on need and not necessarily on a set system or quota as in later periods. The rough proportion of infantry to cavalry in both the army of Romulus and Servius Tullius, effectively ten to one, may represent something like reality – as warfare would have been limited to those rich enough to afford their own equipment and the very rich (possibly the top ten per cent of the army) may very well have utilized horses, as we know these were present in the region. However, given the heavily forested nature of Latium during this period, in contrast to modern day Central Italy, it is questionable how effective cavalry would have been in actual combat – at least as anything resembling a unified force. So it is probably best to consider the number of various troop types and the distribution and use of equipment in the army of this period to be haphazard and largely based on personal choice and preference.

When considering how the army behaved in battle, although there are a number of battle descriptions preserved in the narrative, the vast majority are either so general or so mythologized and full of clearly anachronistic detail that it would be unwise to take them at anything resembling face value. Indeed, most scholars writing about the Roman army during the Regal period have, justifiably, often steered clear of using the more narrative passages in their analyses for these sorts of reasons. However, looking a little more closely, some broad themes do emerge which may shed some light on the situation. Perhaps the most obvious and consistent aspects of early Roman warfare seen in the literature are its open character and individual aspect. Warriors are regularly described engaging in duels and individual combat as part of a fluid battle where movement around the battlefield seems to be both possible and easy. This type of individual combat could (and often did) take the form of a formal duel, as seen with the 'Battle of the Champions' between the Horatii and Curiatii in the reign of Tullus Hostilius.

There happened to be in each of the armies a triplet of brothers, fairly matched in years and strength. It is generally agreed that they were called Horatii and Curiatii. Few incidents in antiquity have been more widely celebrated, yet in spite of its celebrity there is a discrepancy in the accounts as to which nation each belonged. There are authorities on both sides, but I find that the majority give the name of Horatii to the Romans, and my sympathies lead me to follow them. The kings suggested to them that they should each fight on behalf of their country, and where victory rested, there should be the sovereignty. They raised no objection; so the time and place were fixed. But before they engaged a treaty was concluded between the Romans and the Albans, providing that the nation whose representatives proved victorious should receive the peaceable submission of the other. This is the earliest treaty recorded, and as all treaties, however different the conditions they contain, are concluded with the same forms, I will describe the forms with which this one was concluded as handed down by tradition.[14]

Alternatively, and far more commonly, there are numerous references to heroes confronting each other on the battlefield. Most notably there is Romulus defeating the king of the Caenina and winning the *spolia opima* for the first time.

Whilst they were scattered far and wide, pillaging and destroying, Romulus came upon them with an army, and after a brief encounter taught them that anger is futile without strength. He put them to a hasty flight, and following them up, killed their king and despoiled his body; then after slaying their leader took their city at the first assault.[15]

Additionally, there are countless other instances where key figures in the narrative find themselves engaged in combat, as with Mettius Curtius and Hostius Hostilius in the war against the Sabines, or the combat between Brutus and Arruns Tarquin following the removal of Tarquinius Superbus.

> Similarly the enemy's cavalry was in front of his main body, Arruns Tarquin, the king's son, in command; the king himself followed with the legionaries. Whilst still at a distance Arruns distinguished the consul by his escort of lictors; as they drew nearer he clearly recognised Brutus by his features, and in a transport of rage exclaimed, 'That is the man who drove us from our country; see him proudly advancing, adorned with our insignia! Ye gods, avengers of kings, aid me!' With these words, he dug spurs into his horse and rode straight at the consul. Brutus saw that he was making for him. It was a point of honour in those days for the leaders to engage in single combat, so he eagerly accepted the challenge, and they charged with such fury, neither of them thinking of protecting himself, if only he could wound his foe, that each drove his spear at the same moment through the other's shield, and they fell dying from their horses, with the spears sticking in them.[16]

Although these types of duels likely contain a strong mythic element, scholars (most notably Stephen Oakley) have convincingly argued, based on continued evidence for duelling throughout the Republic, that this type of single combat represented a regular aspect of war within the Roman military system and should not be discounted so quickly.[17] The long tradition of the *spolia opima* in particular, which involves the Roman commander successfully defeating the enemy commander in single combat, hints that this type of interaction was not unheard of.

Another intriguing aspect which emerges is the importance of families and clans in warfare. This is something which will be discussed in the next chapter in detail, but it is important to recognize here that families and clans seem to play a much larger role in warfare than the state during this period. On the battlefield, family members are often depicted fighting alongside one another and family structures seem to have formed a viable mechanism for military recruitment, even after the traditional date for the Servian Constitution, as seen through Brutus' recruitment of clan-based forces following the rape of Lucretia or, of course, the famous instance of the private war between the Fabii and Veii in the early Republic and various other similar instances.

Arguably the most interesting and noteworthy difference between the more structural descriptions of the army and the evidence which can be gleaned from the rest of the narrative, is that the bulk of Roman military activity during the Regal period was evidently not centred on state goals or conquest of land, but rather seems to have been largely concerned with raiding for portable wealth. Although all of Rome's *reges* are described as expanding Roman territory militarily and conquering numerous settlements, and indeed the sources suggest that this type of activity was the usual goal of Roman military action, there is no evidence to suggest that any of these 'conquests' resulted in control of settlements or their territory. For instance, Rome's famous victory over Alba Longa under Tullus Hostilius did not result in long-term Roman control over the region, or indeed the land in between the settlements. This 'conquest', like other victories after it during the Regal period, clearly had an immediate impact on the community in terms of loss of life and property but did not seem to result in the attestable creation of an extensive Roman 'kingdom' or 'dominion' over Latium.

This changing understanding of Roman warfare and the increasing absence of a grand strategic vision behind Roman military activity has also led scholars to challenge the literary sources' interpretation of colonization. E.T. Salmon in his great work on the subject, *Roman Colonization Under the Republic*, published in 1970, followed the line of reasoning presented in Livy that Roman colonies planted during the Regal and early Republican periods were strategic in nature, used to secure territorial gains by the state. This approach has increasingly come under fire, however, in recent years as scholars have noted that Rome's Regal colonies were actually never founded following victories and did not seem to maintain a strong political or military link to Rome – and indeed they often went into 'revolt'. All this suggests that Regal colonization should probably not be interpreted as 'Roman expansion', as with the creation of citizen and veteran colonies in later periods, but rather as independent elite initiatives established for a range of other reasons.[18]

Overall then, the narrative for early Roman warfare outside of the various authorial asides, which were likely added during the second and first centuries BC during the expansion of the historical narrative, paints a slightly different picture. Instead of having a grand strategy during this early period, Roman warfare seems to have been directed for short-term gains by powerful warlords who relied heavily on the city's (and region's) clans for manpower. Battles themselves seem to have been a mixture of ambushes, raids and the occasional large scale engagements, but were generally open affairs with a significant amount of duelling and individual combat between aristocrats. The nature of warfare is therefore still extremely tribal and heroic where the state and community concerns seem to play a minimal role.

In many ways this situation actually mirrors what Livy and Dionysius suggest existed with Rome's tribal army under Romulus, although they naturally seem to have envisaged a bit more state control following their expectations based on Rome's late Republican system. Intriguingly though, there is no evidence in the narrative for any changes which might have resulted from the introduction of the Servian Constitution. During the reign of Servius Tullius and the final Tarquin we do not find the expected shift towards large group engagements or formations, state-centred military goals, the emergence of a hoplite ethos in battle, etc. The sources, despite the fact that they clearly envisaged Rome as a conquest-driven city-state, still describe a mode of warfare which was decidedly aristocratic in nature and driven by raiding/booty. Tarquinius Superbus, for instance, is reported as engaging in raiding against Ardea explicitly in order to acquire booty. The same can also be said of the actions of the young Sextus Tarquinius at Gabii and the vast majority of military actions in the early Republic.

Archaeology of Warfare in Archaic Rome

The archaeology for warfare in Latium during the Regal period is unfortunately limited and subject to a range of interpretations, but still provides an interesting parallel to the revised interpretation of the literature. The military equipment discovered in Central Italy dating to the period, largely from Etruria but also found near rich Latin communities like Praeneste, often seems to corroborate the picture of military development presented by Livy and Dionysius. Initial finds of swords, spears, axes and the occasional bits of bronze armour slowly seem to have given way to more complete bronze panoplies in the seventh and sixth centuries BC, often including large circular bronze shields and what appear to be hoplons. This sequence was clearly visible in Etruria, where identifiable hoplons – complete with the central *porpax* and *antilabe* grips, and in some instances with the wooden backing preserved – have been found. Despite the absence of similar evidence from Rome, it was often thought something similar must have been present there, given the strong Etruscan influence on the city during the sixth century BC under the Tarquins.

The key factor in the use of the archaeology to support the literary model was the interpretation of the hoplon and, albeit to a lesser extent, the heavy bronze armour. The mere presence of the Greek-style hoplon was often thought to necessitate densely-packed formations of heavy infantry, simply by virtue of its design. The large circular shield was believed to be too unwieldy for individual combat, while the use of the central *porpax* (a central metal band meant to carry the weight of the shield on the forearm) would have supposedly created an overlap to the left of the bearer which would have been ideally suited to a dense formation. Additionally, the heavy bronze armour which usually accompanied the shields, and particularly the 'closed' bronze helmet, was thought to have limited the sight and movement of a warrior to such a degree that the only practical means of fighting was as part of a dense formation where one only needed to see straight ahead and where movement was limited to a shoving match.

This interpretation of the hoplon and the associated heavy bronze armour has, however, undergone a massive revision in recent years. Led by Hans van Wees and his seminal work, *Greek Warfare: Myths and Realities*, a growing number of scholars have challenged the traditional view and pointed out that in Greece the hoplon and heavy bronze equipment actually grew out of a very individual form of combat prevalent in the Greek 'Dark Ages' (c. 1100–800 BC). Indeed, the closed helmet and full body armour would have arguably been redundant in a dense formation, where the formation itself would have provided the vast majority of the protection. This is something which can be seen during the Classical period of Greek warfare as various pieces of equipment are slowly dropped from the standard panoply until only the shield, spear and helmet are deemed essential in the Athenian phalanx by the mid-fourth century BC, with the minimal armour worn by the soldiers of the *sarissa* phalanx of Philip II and Alexander of Macedon possibly representing the culmination of development. This argument, although by no means universally accepted, would actually turn the interpretation of hoplon and bronze armour finds on its head, as it might suggest the presence of this equipment in fact indicates an individual approach to combat. It naturally does not rule out the use of a phalanx formation as well, but it suggests that the formation may have developed *despite* the heavy equipment instead of *because* of it, likely driven by social forces and not technological determinism.

The development of these models for early Greek warfare has naturally muddied the water quite a bit for early Roman warfare, as it has removed the most obvious reading of the limited finds we have and opened up an entire range of alternative interpretations. Thankfully though, it has also stopped the glossing-over of finds and evidence which did not fit neatly into a mode of warfare which utilized hoplite phalanxes. Most notably this included evidence for a range of different weapons, and particularly the widespread use of axes in military contexts, as axe heads have been found in the vast majority of graves containing other identifiable military equipment and reliefs featuring warriors from Central Italy. There are also a number of bronze shields which were interpreted as hoplons because of their circular shape, but which were clearly never meant to be used in combat as they lacked the wooden backing which provides the ultimate strength – instead the small central handle was attached directly to the bronze sheet which formed the front, creating a beautiful, but ultimately entirely decorative, piece of equipment.

Added to this diverse range of equipment finds are a series of artistic depictions of warriors, again (and unfortunately) almost always found in either burial or explicitly religious contexts, which may shed some additional light on the matter. These include the ubiquitous warrior figurines found in graves throughout Central Italy, tomb and sarcophagus paintings (largely found in Etruria), temple sculptures and vase paintings. All of these types of art defy a clear and detailed interpretation for a number of reasons. First, the artist who created the item may not have been attempting to depict local practice, or indeed anything practical, when creating the work. Archaeologists must assume that the finished piece had some sort of cultural resonance with the local community which ultimately incorporated it into their funerary or religious practice, but what that resonance was is uncertain. For instance, a figurine or vase painting may have depicted a local warrior, a mythic or heroic figure, a god, a Greek warrior, an interpretation of what a Greek warrior looked like, etc. Or it may have merely represented 'wealth'. There are a few constants running through the artistic and iconographic corpus for Central Italy, however, which are consistent enough, and also align with the more concrete military equipment finds, which may be indicative of local norms. These include the regular use of heavy armour on the torso, including both bronze and linen cuirasses, an overall preference for more open helmets and the use of a wide range of weapons, including swords, spears and axes.

There also seems to have been a very strong connection between both military equipment and warrior depictions and elite status. This represents a very early trend in Archaic Central Italy, as seen in the finds from Osteria dell'Osa where weapon deposits in particular have been shown to align with high-status male graves.[19] Although initially the depositions could be argued to represent merely 'wealth', based on the amount of metal and craftsmanship which went into each object (this may help to explain the military equipment found in a few female graves), the increasingly miniaturized and symbolic nature of the finds does suggest that warfare and military equipment had a direct connection to social and political authority. This correlation can also be seen in other graves from around Central Italy, most notably from Castel di Decima and Praeneste in Latium, and many sites, like Tarquinia, in southern Etruria. Warrior figurines and military equipment finds drop off substantially in Latium during the sixth century BC, but the few finds which have been excavated from the sixth and fifth centuries BC – for instance the famous Lanuvium warrior burial, dated to c. 500 BC – suggest a general continuation of practice.

Finally, when looking at the physical remains for warfare in Central Italy, one must also consider fortifications and city defences. For Central Italy, this evidence is puzzling as many communities, including Rome, did invest in fortifications during the seventh and sixth centuries BC , but they were usually simple affairs which only protected the easiest access routes. In Rome, some scholars have suggested that stone blocks found near the Palatine may represent the Archaic 'Wall of Romulus', although this is anything but certain. The first clearly identifiable fortifications at Rome are the *agger* and *fossa* (rampart and ditch) which cut across the

Esquiline plateau, often dated to the sixth century BC based on pottery finds within the fill. Very similar to contemporary fortifications at other Latin sites, this *agger* and *fossa* took advantage of the natural topography of the community and protected the easiest route into the area from the east. The fortifications were extremely limited though and left large areas unprotected. This has led many scholars to suggest that these defences were designed to guard against raids and not as protection from sieges or major assaults. The first walls which were built at Rome which seem to have completely surrounded the city, the so-called 'Servian Walls', were only built in the fourth century BC.

So the final picture we have from the archaeological and artistic evidence for warfare during the Regal period seems to be one of aristocratic dominance. Military equipment and warrior iconography are only found associated with high status graves and adorn temples and tombs which were built by the aristocracy. This does not rule out participation in warfare by members of the lower class as well – but there is no evidence for it either. Additionally, there seemed to be something about military equipment and warrior iconography which resonated with the region's elite as they, or in the case of a burial their family, chose these items and images to identify themselves with.

Conclusions and the power of the *rex*

The evidence for the Roman army during the Regal period is, ultimately then, contradictory. On the one hand we have the explicit testimony of the ancient sources which present a clear and coherent sequence of military development in a series of detailed asides, which envisaged a state-centred tribal army being created under Romulus and transformed into something resembling a civic militia, possibly based on a Greek-style hoplite phalanx, during the reign of Servius Tullius in the sixth century BC. Despite the change in the army's structure and equipment during the sixth century BC, both armies seem to have functioned as an extension of the state's (and *rex*'s) will, in much the same way as the Roman armies of the later Republic. Indeed, Rome's Regal army, at least in these passages, is very clearly depicted as the point of origin and obvious ancestor for the later army and was seen to exhibit many of its key characteristics.

Outside of these few explanatory asides however, the literary evidence paints a picture of an army and a style of warfare that was much more aristocratic and heroic in nature. Far from being based on state-centred aims, warfare was conducted for booty and glory and short-term goals. Armies functioned not as an extension of the state and state policy, but as an extension of a powerful leader's will. Military equipment was, and would remain, personal property and the type of equipment used in Archaic Central Italy is increasingly interpreted as being best suited for individual, and not group, action. Even the construction of fortifications is unlikely to have involved and included the full community.

The key issue, then, is the connection between the powerful clan leader, the army and the community – a power that the Roman's associated with the grant of *imperium*.

The power of *imperium* is what bound a powerful clan leader, or warlord, to the community of Rome and to the army. Although we naturally have extremely limited and problematic information for this power in the Archaic period, as all of our evidence comes from later periods when *imperium* may have changed and evolved, it seems to have given an external leader the power to control, command and effectively integrate the members of the community into his own clan-based military model. A *rex*, via *imperium*, represented a powerful father figure to those in his army, with all of the power that a Roman *paterfamilias* would have wielded – including the power of life or death and the ability to judge those under his control.

This relationship clearly had power both ways, as the inclusion of community members in the army and retinue of a warlord would have changed the character of the power dynamic within. Additionally, the fact that *imperium* was granted by the community, with the *comitia curiata* effectively putting themselves under the warlord's command and power, also suggests that they retained a certain amount of power and control in the relationship and could possibly remove themselves from it if needed. Fundamentally though, Rome's army in the Regal period seems to have represented the result of an integration with a previously existing mode of aristocratic, clan-based warfare and military model, which actually continued to exist alongside the city's armies well into the Republican period.

Chapter 2

The Power of the Clans

There are very few points upon which modern historians of early Rome can agree. However, no matter which interpretation of the sources one adopts, or which model of early Roman society one believes in, it is clear that aristocratic clans and families played a major role in the warfare and politics of both the city of Rome and the region as a whole. Although Rome's historians, writing in the late Republic and early Empire, clearly envisaged a cohesive Roman society with an active and vocal citizen body which included both the plebeians and the patrician elite, the narrative of early Roman history down to the end of the fourth century BC is driven almost entirely by the actions of powerful clan leaders. From Rome's early wars to the transition from a monarchy to a Republic and the events of the fifth century BC, early Roman history is effectively a narrative of clan competition. Add to this the extensive evidence for hierarchical clan-based structures present in the archaeological record going back to at least the eighth century BC, and the image becomes very clear – all of Central Italian society, and not just Rome, seems to have been dominated by powerful clans and their leaders. However, the exact nature of this power and its relationship to the Roman state, and the Roman army, is far more problematic.

Again returning to the traditional interpretation of events, the literary sources (unsurprisingly given when they were written) seem to suggest that the situation in early Rome resembled the situation in the late Republic, where powerful families vied with each other for power, but always within an overarching, state-based structure. Clans and clan leaders competed for public office, status in the community and control of the army, but all as part of a 'game' played within the confines of Rome's socio-political setting. Or at least that was the general idea. Given the events of the late Republic and the seeming disregard for the 'rules' seen in the actions of men like Sulla, Caesar and even Augustus, it is debatable whether this model even held sway at the time when Livy and Dionysius were writing. And when looking at the events of early Rome it is clear that this model is far too simple for this time period as well, as a number of events from the late Regal period and early Republic exemplify. The so-called 'private war' between the Fabii and Veii in the 470s BC, the movement of powerful families like the Claudi and even the development of Rome's magistrates – the transition from the *rex* to the early consuls/praetors, to the consular tribunes and then to a new and reinvigorated consulship – have all defied explanation in a model where Rome's elite competed within a cohesive, state-centred environment.

In recent years, scholars have argued that if the powerful clans of Rome, and Central Italy more generally, are freed from the traditional, rigid, state-based mode of interaction, things start to make a bit more sense. When the anachronistic assumptions of Rome's late Republican historians are removed, and particularly those concerning the goals and allegiances of Central Italy's Archaic elite (i.e. that they may not have cared about their position in Rome quite as much as their late Republican counterparts), a new and far simpler picture emerges. Rome, including her political and military *apparati*, becomes just one more avenue or aspect within a larger game for social and economic power within the region. Although Rome was a large and growing community, located in a strategic position at the crossing point of the Tiber, becoming a major player in Roman society and Roman politics was clearly not the only, or indeed the primary, means to acquire power and social prestige during the Archaic period. The region's clans can be seen to compete in a much broader sense, which puts a whole new spin on the nature of warfare in the region.

Latium's Clans in the Archaic Period

Perhaps the largest shift which has occurred in recent years in the scholarship relating to early Rome has been the transition from a model of Central Italy dominated by powerful communities – the thirty cities of the 'Latin League' and the twelve cities of the 'Etruscan League' – toward a model where urban centres shared power with a number of mobile, rural clans. The impetus for this shift has come largely from the field of archaeology. Although by no means conclusive, the archaeological evidence has increasingly been interpreted as indicating the presence of powerful kinship-based groups which interacted with the local communities, often on a regular basis, but whose existence and identity were not entirely reliant upon them. Often based in rural areas, the groups do seem to have focused on different communities as their social, cultural and economic interests developed during the Archaic period, although they were also more than happy to shift this focus if the situation became unfavourable. Some vital questions still remain though, most notably, what did these early clans look like? Christopher Smith's 2006 book, *The Roman Clan: The* Gens *from Ancient Ideology to Modern Anthropology*, represents the most complete attempt at answering the basic questions 'what was a "clan" in Archaic Central Italy?' and 'how does this affect our understanding of early Roman society?' Unfortunately, the answers to both questions are not entirely straightforward ones. As Smith notes in the first chapter, 'the idea that the *gens* [clan] had a single form which even ideally might be recovered is one which this book explicitly rejects'. Rather than a stable institution, the Roman clan seems to have been an evolving mechanism for identifying oneself which existed outside of, albeit alongside, other mechanisms like citizenship and community identification. Cicero offers the following definition of members of a Roman clan, or *gens*, in the late Republic:

Again: '*gentiles* in relations to each other are those who share the same *nomen*.' That is not enough. 'Those who are born from freeborn citizens.' That too is not enough. 'Of whose ancestors no-one has served in slavery.' There is still something missing. 'Who have not suffered *capitis diminutio*.' Perhaps that is enough. For I see that Scaevola the *pontifex* has added nothing to this definition.[1]

Although admittedly a bit cryptic, in this definition the key aspect of clan membership is sharing a *nomen*, which is the second name in the typical Roman three-name system – i.e. the 'Julius' in 'Gaius Julius Caesar'. This particular part of a Roman name was even called the *nomen gentilicium* or 'clan name' by various authors. However, as Cicero notes, merely sharing a *nomen* did not make one part of a *gens* or clan. Freed slaves often took the name of their former master as a type of *nomen* and these were clearly not considered part of a *gens* in the late Republic – although their position in earlier periods is a little more ambiguous. Additionally, Cicero's last qualification, not suffering *capitis diminutio* – which effectively means a loss of citizenship and citizen rights – is unlikely to have meant much in an Archaic context when the idea of Roman citizenship itself seems to have been reasonably flexible.

It is an oft remarked fact that Rome's earliest figures seem to have had only one name – Romulus, Remus, Numa, etc. – and only as the Regal period wore on did the use of the *nomen*, or second name, become the norm. This feature is not found simply in the late Republican histories of Rome, but is also supported by the epigraphic record for Latium, where a sixth century BC start date for the regular use of the *nomen* has been suggested. This indicates that while in earlier periods one might have simply had a personal name, by the sixth century BC Central Italy's system of clans seems to have been formalized enough that individuals were often identified using a clan-based descriptor as well. The *cognomen*, or third name in the three-name system used to indicate a particular branch of a clan/family, seems to have only become widespread in the third century BC, although there is some evidence for limited use earlier.

The size and composition of Rome's early clans likely varied quite a bit. By the late Republic, the sources suggest that there were over 1,000 *nomena* in use in Rome, although whether that indicates 1,000 clans is still debated. We do know, however, that even in the earliest periods there were recognized groups of both powerful and weak clans (*gentes maiores* and *minores*) and it is likely that there existed a number of even lesser *gentes*, which probably barely warranted the name. The question of how a clan became more powerful is also a tricky one to answer. Obviously one could increase in size by having more children, although if this was the only mechanism used to increase the power of a *gens* it would be an incredibly slow and unwieldy one. Three other mechanisms may have also been used in Archaic Central Italy. The first may have been through the acquisition and later freeing of slaves. As noted above, a freed slave would often adopt the *nomen* of his master and, while not representing a fully fledged member of a clan, may have represented part of their larger sphere of influence. Intriguingly though, Central Italian clans seem to have been able to use social bonds to increase their power as well. One of the clearest examples of this, which evidently continued down into the late Republic and indeed Imperial periods, is through the use of clients (*clientes*).

The patron–client relationship seems to have had a very long tradition in Rome, being attested in the earliest Roman law code – the fifth century BC 'Laws of the Twelve Tables' – and played a key role in the early narrative of the city. Given that the relationship continued down into the more historical periods, and given the tendency for Rome's historians to assume that institutions like this did not change over time (sometimes even when there is clear evidence to the contrary!), it is hard to say anything concrete about the early relationship. However, the bond was something which was recognized by law and clearly represented an important and formal connection between one individual and another. Clients and followers are consistently mentioned as part of the overall strength of a clan and even seem to have moved and settled with them in some instances.

In addition to clients, there is increasing evidence for another type of bond used to expand the power of a clan which has particular relevance for early warfare – the addition of a 'sword brother', or *sodalis*. This is another relationship which had an early origin and remained a part of Roman society/culture down into the Empire, although here the evidence for change and development is much more pronounced. While the patron–client relationship seems to have retained many of its core characteristics, the *sodal* bond seems to have moved from something which existed largely in the military sphere to a religious or priestly affiliation. By the late Republic and early Empire, the term *sodales* – often translated as 'follower', 'brother' or 'companion' – was usually used to refer to members of a priestly fraternity like the *sodales augustales*. But early literary evidence, most notably from the third century BC playwright Plautus (our earliest extant Roman literary source), sheds some additional light on the matter. Plautus used a number of different words to refer to friends or companions in his plays, including '*sodalis*', '*amicus*' and '*vicine*' (meaning neighbour). However, the title *sodalis* seems to have required certain characteristics, as they were always a male, often of a similar age and there was usually some sort of military or martial overtone involved. There is also increasing evidence from archaeology to support the existence of 'sword brothers' in Central Italian clans. The famous Lapis Satricanus, a fragmentary inscription found on a stone which was reused in the wall of a late sixth century BC temple in the Latin site of Satricum, contains a dedication to the god Marmars (likely a version of the later Roman god of war Mars) by the *sodales* of a Populos Valesios (the actual inscriptions reads ... *IEI STETERAI POPLIOSIO VALESIOSIO SUODALES MAMARTEI)*. The meaning of this inscription is obviously hotly debated, but it suggests the presence of a group of individuals, likely men, who followed a leader named Populos Valesios (possibly the Roman noble Publicola) and had an association with a deity which was later associated with warfare.

Additionally, there is evidence from the early Iron Age cemetery at Osteria dell'Osa, near the site of Gabii, which may be relevant. Excavated during the 1970s and 1980s by Anna Maria Bietti Sestieri, the cemetery represents the most important site in Latium for the early Iron Age.[2] In the cemetery, Bietti Sestieri has identified the beginnings of clan groups – visible in their distinct burial patterns – which focus on one or two high status burials at the centre. Outside of these high status graves at the centre there are rough, concentric zones of graves which featured male burials associated with military equipment, followed by female graves, lower status male graves, etc. This was thought to indicate a hierarchical, patrilineal clan-based structure with a focus on military equipment and military activity as a key feature of social status. At the periphery of these groups, however, she found a few anomalous graves. Although clearly connected to the larger clan-based grave organization, these graves did not fit the pattern. While one would have expected to find very low status graves in this position, these graves seem to have contained high status warriors. One possible explanation for these graves would be the presence of *sodales*, high-status warriors or 'sword brothers', associated with a clan but not necessarily part of it. These may have been the Archaic Italian equivalent of Beowulf's companions or King Arthur's 'Knights of the Round Table'.

Increasingly, the scholarly perception of Archaic Central Italy is therefore of a region dominated by powerful, hierarchical, militarized clans. Generally based in rural areas. These clans were also evidently quite mobile and able to move around as their situation dictated. Indeed there is ample evidence in both the literary sources and the archaeology for these clans moving around quite a bit, with literary examples like the Claudii arriving in Rome at the end of the sixth century BC and the Tarquins arriving a century earlier, while evidence from Osteria dell'Osa indicates that the clans who buried their members there did not always live in the region but most likely maintained the site as a ritual area. This begs the question, why would these clans move around? A range of reasons are likely to have influenced their decisions, but it is probable that economics played a major role. First, there is strong evidence to suggest that many of these clans were engaged in what is known as 'limited transhumance pastoralism' during the Archaic period, which involves the raising of animals which require movement to different grazing pastures throughout the course of the year. Second, it is likely that many of these clans were also involved in the increasingly lucrative trade running between the Etruscan cities of the north and the new Greek colonies in the south of Italy. While this naturally did not require large-scale movement on their part, it did mean that they were often associated with the main travel routes through the region. This mobility and association with a range of cultures meant that the clans present in Latium should really be considered regional entities. Although clearly aware of and often interacting with the communities dotted across the Latin landscape, like Rome, the regional clans seem to have existed as part of a slightly different and much larger world.

Latium's Communities in the Archaic Period

Turning now to Central Italy and Latium's various communities, if the region's powerful clans existed largely outside of them, who lived inside? A surprisingly wide variety of people, it seems. According to the narrative of Romulus' foundation of Rome, the city's first inhabitants were a mixture of cultures and represented the full spectrum of Central Italian society, with runaway slaves, asylum-seekers, merchants, local farmers and of course Romulus' more aristocratic followers. Dionysius offers the following description:

In the sixteenth generation after the Trojan war the Albans united both these places into one settlement, surrounding them with a wall and a ditch. For until then there were only folds for cattle and sheep and quarters of the other herdsmen, as the land round about yielded plenty of grass, not only for winter but also for summer pasture, by reason of the rivers that refresh and water it. The Albans were a mixed nation composed of Pelasgians, of Arcadians, of the Epeans who came from Elis, and, last of all, of the Trojans who came into Italy with Aeneas, the son of Anchises and Aphroditê, after the taking of Troy. It is probable that a barbarian element also from among the neighbouring peoples or a remnant of the ancient inhabitants of the place was mixed with the Greek. But all these people, having lost their tribal designations, came to be called by one common name, Latins, after Latinus, who had been king of this country. The walled city, then, was built by these tribes in the four hundred and thirty-second year after the taking of Troy, and in the seventh Olympiad.[3]

Livy, on the other hand, offers a slightly less favourable but still multifaceted description:

Next, lest his big City should be empty, Romulus resorted to a plan for increasing the inhabitants which had long been employed by the founders of cities, who gather about them an obscure and lowly multitude and pretend that the earth has raised up sons to them. In the place which is now enclosed, between the two groves as you go up the hill, he opened a sanctuary. Thither fled, from the surrounding peoples, a miscellaneous rabble, without distinction of bond or free, eager for new conditions; and these constituted the first advance in power towards that greatness at which Romulus aimed.[4]

The earliest archaeological evidence from the site of Rome supports this mixed composition and suggests a collection of small, independent settlements were located on Rome's hills – particularly the Palatine – which gradually unified during the seventh and sixth centuries BC. This process of unification is generally associated with the filling-in of the forum area between the hills. This area had traditionally been marshy and unsuitable for habitation, although there is evidence for a few huts in the early Iron Age and it was evidently used as a cemetery by the communities on the surrounding hills in the early periods of the site's inhabitation. During the course of the seventh and sixth century BC, however, it was gradually filled-in with the land level being raised by several metres in some areas to create a communal space – perhaps driven in part by the use of the local clay deposits and an expansion in local pottery production. Burials soon shifted out of the forum to the Esquiline hill and a number of more permanent structures were built in the forum area.

The growth of Rome in the Archaic period can be directly linked with the growth of trade between the Etruscan cities of Etruria and the Greek colonies of Magna Graecia. The region of Latium represented something of a thoroughfare for this trade. Latium was not particularly rich in terms of natural resources, unlike Etruria to the north, and with its powerful and warlike clans and dearth of good harbours, unlike the bay of Naples to the south, the Greeks did not colonize it. But trade between these two groups often passed through the region and the communities situated on the main trade routes, which included a coastal route and an inland route along the Sacco-Liri river valley, began to thrive. This included the sites of Satricum, Ardea, Lavinium, Praeneste and Gabii to name but a few. Any communities not located on these trade routes quickly declined and fell into obscurity, the best examples being the settlements on the Alban Hills in central Latium. The communities in the Alban hills had represented the hub of early settlement activity, but soon became economic backwaters in the Archaic period. Rome, conveniently situated on a major choke point for this trade at the best crossing point of the Tiber, benefited more than most from this trade and resultant population growth.

The people brought to Rome and Latium's other communities by this trade came from across the Mediterranean. Inscriptions, shrines and votive offerings all suggest that a number of Greeks, Etruscans and Phoenicians made their way through the region's burgeoning urban centres during the Archaic period, with many likely deciding to stay and set up shop for at least a limited time. It is likely that the region's clans also interacted with the growing urban areas, trading for items and selling livestock at locations like Rome's *Forum Boarium*, the city's ancient cattle market. But while some of these groups may have settled in the communities, many seem to have been largely transient. The core population in sites like Rome, Praeneste, Gabii and other Latin communities was made up of a few more sedentary and agriculturally-minded Latins. Emerging out of the same culture which had given birth to the region's clans, the urban populations in Latium seem to have been much more egalitarian in nature. Based around smaller groups, most likely nuclear families, these men and women lacked the strong, hierarchical framework of the *gentes* and instead buried their dead with much less order and often with far fewer grave goods. Although some individuals and groups, for instance at the Latin community of Praeneste, seem to have acquired quite a bit of wealth from the trade running through the region, the majority of the urban population was likely primarily concerned with agriculture and represented small-scale farmers, working small farmsteads near the communities which had been carved out of the dense forests which covered most of Central Italy at that time.

The multifaceted group formed by the farmers, merchants and other urban-based tradesmen/industrialists in Rome is likely to have represented the ancestors of the so-called 'plebeians' of the Republican period. Although it is highly unlikely that they identified as such during the Archaic period, during the early Republic the plebeian group seems to have encompassed all those living in the community who were not associated with the powerful patrician (i.e. patriarchal) clans. Given the lack of a strong pre-existing hierarchy or power structure, the urban communities still needed some form of government and likely utilized a basic assembly with a few limited term magistrates. In Rome, this is likely represented by the archaic *curiae* and the curiate assembly. Although modern historians cannot agree on even the composition or character of the early *curiae* (the famous historian Arnaldo Momigliano once noted in frustration that 'we would know how the Archaic Roman institutions worked if we knew what the *Curiae* were'[5]), it is clear that they represented the basic administrative units of the urban population of Rome and the curiate assembly was in charge of the basic running of the community. This included the election of magistrates, issues to do with family law (a power which was preserved even into the late Republic) and – most famously – the ability to grant/confirm *imperium*. There also seem to have been minor limited term magistrates associated with the *curiae* which went by the titles *tribunus* and *curio*.

This leads us to the ways in which the clans of Central Italy interacted with the community. As with many things relating to early Rome, how the powerful rural clans interacted with the urban communities is far from certain. As mentioned previously, it is likely that the clans passed through the communities as part of the trade running though Latium, engaging in some of the north/south activity between the Greek and Etruscans and perhaps taking part in a separate east/west, or highland/lowland, trade pattern based on the movement of livestock. Of more interest though are the clans which decided, for one reason or another, to base themselves around communities like Rome, or indeed within it. How did these powerful, patriarchal, hierarchical clans interact with the more egalitarian communities? There were probably countless informal ways in which the members of these two groups interacted, but in formal and political terms, the key avenues were through the institution of the senate and the power of *imperium* as wielded by the *rex* (often translated simply as 'king', although this is not entirely correct) and later the consuls/ praetors.

The senate is by far the easier of these two to interpret. In the late Republic, it represented a council of elders whose power was often unofficial but who controlled Rome by virtue of their immense wealth and family-based connections. By that period, membership in the senate was partly timocratic, or wealth-based, and partly determined by social factors, all of which were controlled by the censors. In the Regal period and early Republic, however, the senate was likely nothing more than a collection of powerful clan leaders (*patres*) who happened to be based around Rome and met from time to time to discuss matters of mutual interest. Much of the evidence, even though it was written during a time when the senate was a formal and incredibly powerful body, suggests that this group was largely informal during this period. It is only with the gradual introduction of new members, likely members of the plebeians who may have gone by the title *conscripti* (not being *patres* of *gentes* themselves), that the body took on its more formal overtones. This early senate therefore likely exercised a very informal brand of power – indicating what these powerful individuals and their followers thought and wanted, but leaving the running of the community up to those who lived there.

The main point of intersection was the grant of *imperium* given to the *rex*, and later the consuls/praetors. Despite the fact that the nature of *imperium* has been hotly debated since the early nineteenth century, the marked absence of scholarship focusing on the Archaic period reveals our almost complete lack of knowledge about this key period. However, here is roughly what we do know – or think we know. *Imperium* was granted to (or confirmed on) the *rex* by a *lex* or law passed by the *comitia curiata*, as this practice was maintained under the Republic – despite the fact that the consuls and praetors were elected by another assembly. At its core, *imperium* seems to have represented the right to command Rome's armies, although it may have included other powers as well – this is not entirely certain. However, *imperium* did not indicate a monopoly on warfare by the *rex* (or later consuls/praetors), as there are countless references to individuals without *imperium* leading military ventures from Rome down into the fourth century BC. We also know that *imperium* was somehow connected with a religious aspect, *auspicium*, and may have carried with it a number of ritual insignia, including the presence of lictors, use of the *curule* chair, etc. It also seems to have been connected with the right to celebrate a triumph in Rome. We can also say quite a lot about those who were initially granted *imperium*. The early *reges* of Rome were all outsiders to the city who seem to have had substantial power bases in their own right – in other words, they were members of the region's powerful, clan-based aristocracy. Indeed, it is an interesting and often commented-upon quirk of early Roman society that they seem to have had no problem granting *imperium* to individuals from different cultural or ethnic groups, as Rome's *reges* included Latins, Sabines and Etruscans (possibly of Greek descent). There are a number of possible reasons for this openness with regards to *imperium*, not the least of which is the diverse nature of Roman society at this time. However, it is possible that this openness may also relate to the nature of *imperium* itself. The open character of *imperium* continued under the Republic as it was generally granted to powerful clan leaders, who often had only a passing connection to the city itself – either just arriving or leaving soon after holding office. Indeed, Rome's aristocracy only settled down into a coherent group towards the end of the fifth century BC – a phenomenon known as the 'closing of the *patriciate*', first identified by the historian Gaetano De Sanctis in the early twentieth century. Although the regularity with which *imperium* was granted to 'outsiders' and 'newcomers' to the community may represent a fluke or problem with our sources, it might also suggest something about the purpose of *imperium*. As noted above, the community of Rome during the Archaic period seems to have been composed of a roughly egalitarian mix of peoples who seem to have lacked a strong hierarchical structure and, although they were increasingly wealthy, did not seem to have represented a particularly militarized body. However, the rest of the region was full of powerful, organized, mobile and evidently warlike clans, whose wealth was based on portable goods. It is possible that the office of the *rex* and the grant of *imperium* represented a contract between the community and powerful clan leader to act as a protector. In exchange for some level of control over the community, the *rex* and his followers would commit to safeguarding the community and its interests. So perhaps it was something akin to the patron-client relationship which existed later in Rome, as opposed to the modern monarchical models which are often imposed.

The Roman *Gentes*

One of the most common misconceptions concerning the *reges* and the powerful clans of Rome during this period is that they were Roman – or at least 'Roman' in the same way that Rome's late Republican clans and families were. The city of Rome in the Archaic age was a large and sophisticated city with increasingly impressive structures – most notably temples – and infrastructure. Sitting astride the main trade route between the Etruscan north and Greek south, it was a very powerful and important community, and as such many individuals, families and clans seem to have been drawn towards it – caught in its 'gravitational pull'. But despite its sophistication, the idea of Roman citizenship and indeed the concept of 'being Roman' seem to have lagged behind.

For members of the urban community who lacked a strong clan connection, being Roman would have likely meant being part of a *curia* and participating in the *comitia curiata*. As already noted, we still do not quite understand what the Archaic *curiae* were, but they seem to have been associated with various geographic locations within the city and membership may have been based, at least partly, on where you lived. So what would happen if you moved? Would you also change your *curiae*? And what would happen if you left Rome altogether? The answers to these questions are unfortunately impossible to know for certain, but there is strong circumstantial evidence to suggest that once one left Rome, your connection to the community was also severed. Being Roman meant living in Rome – and this was particularly true for the elite.

Early Roman history is full of stories of elites changing their allegiance or 'citizenship', if it can be called that, simply by changing their location. This movement between communities, and sometimes even tribal or ethnic units, is typically couched in terms of 'exile' or 'banishment' (as Rome's later historians likely struggled to understand why anyone would leave Rome!) but may have also reflected personal preference. From the arrival of the various *reges* and their followers in Rome and Sextus Tarquinius' stint in Gabii, to the movement of the Claudii in the early years of the Republic and Coriolanus' exile from and return to Rome with an army of Volscians, there are numerous explicit examples of elites moving from community to community with little or no loss of power. As soon as a group arrived in a new community, they often immediately took up a position of authority which suggests that their real power and prestige lay in something outside of the political apparatus of the community. These elites and their clans were powerful in their own right, and merely used Rome (and the other Latin communities) as an avenue to express and increase that power. But, quite apart from the situation which existed in the late Republic – and which our late Republican historians assumed must be the case earlier – Rome was neither the source of, nor essential for, their power.

Rome was, in many ways, simply another Central Italian community – just one of many growing urban centres which dotted the landscape in the Archaic age. With hindsight we know she gradually grew in power and eventually came to dominate both the region and the Mediterranean, but in the Archaic period she was just another stop along the main route north/south in Central Italy. Indeed, despite her key location on the Tiber, both the literature and archaeology suggest she was not necessarily the most dominant or important community either. Unfortunately, the archaeological record for Rome itself during this period is incredibly thin, largely because of the constant inhabitation of the site and the ephemeral nature of the evidence for this period, but when comparing the few finds we do have, including graves, habitation remains and ultimately temple foundations, it was only during the sixth century BC that Rome gradually became more physically impressive than her local rivals. Looking at the communities which represent Rome's rivals in the Regal period as a comparison - sites like Gabii, Ardea and Praeneste, for whom the archaeological record is a bit more abundant – we see surprisingly small communities who apparently competed successfully with Rome for power. Add to this the almost constant low-level warfare which Rome engaged in during the sixth and fifth centuries BC, with only limited success during this period, and one gets a distinct sense of parity in the region.

This parity between Rome and the other urban centres in Latium during the Archaic period has increasingly broken down the myth of 'Roman exceptionalism'. Although the city eventually grew to prominence and dominance, she was not always the powerful centre to which all roads must lead. Despite being one of the larger communities and increasingly attractive to both powerful clans and merchants, it seems clear that she was not the only option for those clans and elites looking to make their name. Further, although participating in Roman politics and becoming the *rex* or consul did have some advantages, given that the true source of power lay outside of the city's political structure, it is likely that much of the competition between these elites remained extramural as well.

The extramural nature of elite power and interests can be seen in a number of different areas, some of which will be discussed in later sections of this book, but perhaps the clearest indication can be found in how the clans were eventually integrated into Roman society via the Tribal Assembly. Lily Ross Taylor's study of Rome's voting districts, originally published in 1960, remains the key work on this subject. As Taylor noted at the start of her discussion of Rome's rural tribes, these groupings were clearly based on existing *gentes* and their locations relative to Rome:

The sixteen old rural tribes with *gens* names were, in alphabetical order: *Aemelia*, Camilia, *Claudia, Cornelia, Fabia*, Galeria, *Horatia*, Lemonia, *Menenia, Papiria*, Pollia, Pupinia, *Romilia, Sergia*, Voltina, and *Voturia*. Ten of these *gentes*, all italicized in the list, are represented among the chief magistrates of the first century of the republic.[6]

All of these *gentes*, or clans, occupied distinct areas outside of Rome and, in at least one instance (the Claudii), had only arrived in the final years of the sixth century BC.

Unfortunately it is still not entirely clear when these tribal divisions were formalized. The traditional interpretation, given by Livy and Dionysius, is that they were created as part of the reforms of Servius Tullius and functioned alongside the centuries and the Centuriate Assembly. This sixth century BC date for the creation of the tribal organization, however, has drawn almost constant criticism for a number of reasons (most notably, as with the Centuriate Assembly, what function did they serve at this early date?) and various alternative models have been put forward. Even the Romans knew that the tribes and the Tribal Assembly had evolved over time with a number of new tribes being added over the course of the fifth and fourth centuries BC. Although a number of different options are possible, perhaps the most attractive model is the creation of a formal tribal structure sometime in the 440s BC, as this was the time period when the assembly gained real power as both a legislative body and the body which elected quaestors, and also the point of origin for the censorship, a magistracy which was tasked in part with delineating these groups. This period also coincides with the so-called 'closing of the *patriciate*' in the late fifth century BC, the gradual locking down of power by a small collection of powerful *gentes* – unsurprisingly by families which bear the same names as the early tribes. But it is worthwhile noting that the magistrates of the early Republic, just like *reges* before them, came from clans who were based outside of Rome. Additionally, despite the sources suggesting that these groups were static and stationary from the sixth century BC, it is clear that there was at least some movement and fluidity amongst these groups well into the fifth century BC as the literature suggests clans moved in and out of Rome's orbit for a range of reasons.

Central Italian Warlords

As noted above, Livy, Dionysius and the other historians writing in the late Roman Republic clearly envisaged Rome's early *gens*-based elite as engaging in competition following the same rules and norms of the late Republican elite with which they were familiar – all participating in a political 'game' focused on the city of Rome where all the players were, at their core, 'Roman'. In this model, warfare represented just another aspect of the 'game' where the various clans sought to increase both their own power and that of the community. But what happens when we re-evaluate the role and position of the clans, particularly as they relate to warfare, given a scholarly model which suggests that clan power was largely extramural in nature and their relationship to the community was often fluid and ephemeral? In other words, what happens to our understanding of Roman warfare when both the commanders, and very possibly a large portion of the army itself, have very little connection to the community? Increasingly, this has meant transforming what were often thought of as Roman politicians, who sometimes served as generals, into Central Italian 'warlords', who sometimes engaged in Roman politics. The key difference in this new model is the ultimate source of power in Rome, which has seen a gradual shift from the state toward the clan, and a resultant shift in both the nature of command and the army.

The idea of 'warlords' in early Rome, often called *condottieri* by modern scholars (a term which is derived from Italian warlords of the late Middle Ages), is not a new one. As already noted, many of Rome's *reges* were often seen as warlords prior to coming to Rome, with one of the more interesting stories concerning this being reported by the Emperor Claudius and preserved on the famous Tablet of Lyon:

> And according to the Roman sources Servius Tullius had as a mother a prisoner of war, Ocresia; according to the Etruscans he had been the faithful companion of Caelius Vivenna and took part in his adventures, and later, when he was driven out by a change of fortune, he left Etruria with all the surviving troops of Caelius and seized the Caeliian hill, which thus takes its name from his leader Caelius, and after changing his name (for his Etruscan name was Mastarna) he was given the name I have already mentioned, and became king, to the very great advantage of the state. Then, after the behaviour of Tarquinius Superbus came to be hated by our city – and not only his behaviour but that of his sons – the people obviously became tired of monarchy, and the administration of state was transferred to the consuls, who were annual magistrates.[7]

In this version of events, Servius Tullius is associated with a famous Central Italian hero, Mastarna – whose actions are also depicted on the walls of the Francois tomb from Vulci – who, along with the Vibenna brothers, is reported as travelling across Central Italy with a group of warriors and eventually setting himself up as the *rex* in Rome. Macstarna/Servius Tullius' source of power is clearly based on his group of followers and his position in Rome is merely a by-product of this. Indeed, as many scholars have noted over the past 100 years, Livy and Dionysius of Halicarnassus regularly describe powerful clan leaders engaging in warfare outside of the bounds of the state and, in a few troubling instances, in a 'grey area' where private and public seem to overlap. The most obvious example of this is the so-called 'private war' between the Fabii and Veii during the early 470s BC. Livy records the initiation of the war in 479 BC:

But the Veientes inflicted a defeat on the Romans owing to the rashness of the other consul; and the army would have been destroyed if Caeso Fahius had not come, in the nick of time, to its rescue. Thenceforward there was neither peace nor war with the Veientes, but something very like freebooting. In the face of the Roman legions they would retreat into their city; when they perceived the legions to be withdrawn they would make raids upon the fields, evading war by a semblance of peace, and peace in turn by war. Hence it was impossible either to let the whole matter go or to end it. Other wars, too, were immediately threatening – like the one with the Aequi and the Volsci, who would observe peace only so long as the suffering involved in their latest defeat was passing away – or were soon to be begun, by the always hostile Sabines and all Etruria. But the enmity of the Veientes, persistent rather than perilous, and issuing in insults oftener than in danger, kept the Romans in suspense, for they were never permitted to forget it or to turn their attention elsewhere. Then the Fabian clan went before the senate, and the consul said, speaking for the clan: 'A standing body of defenders rather than a large one is required, Conscript Fathers, as you know, for the war with Veii. Do you attend to the other wars, and assign to the Fabii the task of opposing the Veientes. We undertake that the majesty of the Roman name shall be safe in that quarter. It is our purpose to wage this war as if it were our own family feud, at our private costs: the state may dispense with furnishing men and money for this cause.' The thanks of the Fathers were voted with enthusiasm. The consul came out from the senate-house, and escorted by a column of the Fabii, who had halted in the vestibule of the curia while awaiting the senate's decision, returned to his house. After receiving the command to present themselves armed next day at the consul's threshold, they dispersed to their homes.[8]

This narrative is therefore of an elected consul, imbued with *imperium* and able to lead Rome's state-based armies in battle, offering to lead a private, clan-based force against the community of Veii. The Fabii are apparently reasonably successful in this war, at least for the first couple of years, before being ambushed by the Veientines at the Cremera River in 477 BC and famously being slaughtered, almost to the man.

This narrative has caused scholars endless headaches for a number of reasons. First, there are naturally problems with the reliability of this story. The loss of 300 Fabii in 477 BC clearly mirrors the defeat of the 300 Spartans at Thermopylae in 480 BC and it has been argued that this narrative, likely derived from the family history of Fabius Pictor, served the dual function of glorifying his own family and explaining the sudden decline in power of the Fabian *gens* in the middle of the fifth century BC. However, on a more fundamental level, if one believes the basic structure of the narrative, it clearly indicates that the state did not have a monopoly on warfare during the early Republic and that private, clan-based actions were possible. Additionally, the success of the Fabii against Veii, which had recently defeated a Roman army, hints that these clan-based forces were possibly quite formidable and may have rivalled Rome's state-based armies. Finally, it also hints at a grey area in Rome's military system, where a consul with *imperium* felt it acceptable and indeed noble to lead a private force into battle. Based on this narrative, Rome's consuls could also be warlords with their own armies, in addition to the state-based forces they seem to have had command over.

The narrative of the Fabii against Veii is not the only instance of private warfare and private armies in Rome's early history either. The 'rebellion' of Appius Herdonius represents another. Livy records that Herdonius was a Sabine who attacked Rome in 460 BC with a private army and captured the Capitoline hill. As Livy reports:

> Exiles and slaves to the number of twenty-five hundred, led by
> Appius Herdonius, the Sabine, came by night and seized the Capitol

and the Citadel. They at once put to the sword those in the Citadel who refused to conspire and take up arms with them. Some escaped in the confusion and ran down terror-stricken into the Forum. Alternating cries were heard, 'To arms!' and 'The enemy is in the City!'[9]

The use of the term 'exiles' in this passage is an interesting one, as it suggests a connection between the force and Rome. It also perhaps calls to mind the narrative of Coriolanus, who marched on Rome only a few years previously with a foreign force, despite the fact that he had only recently been exiled from Rome himself, hinting that he had taken his power (and likely his followers) with him.[10] And moving even further in history, even as late as the early fourth century BC we have warbands being created through personal and family connections, as with the force of A. Postuimius and L. Iulius in the lead-up to the Gallic sack of Rome. As Livy reports:

A. Postumius and L. Julius raised a force, not by a regular levy – for they were obstructed by the tribunes of the plebs – but consisting mostly of volunteers whom they had induced by strong appeals to come forward. With this they advanced by cross marches through the territory of Caere and surprised the Tarquinians as they were returning heavily laden with booty. They slew great numbers, stripped the whole force of their baggage, and returned with the recovered possessions from their farms to Rome. Two days were allowed for the owners to identify their property; what was unclaimed on the third day, most of it belonging to the enemy, was sold 'under the spear', and the proceeds distributed amongst the soldiers.[11]

So even the literary sources, which explicitly espoused a state-centred approach to warfare, still offer us numerous examples of warlords and warbands functioning in the region, and based in or around the city of Rome, until at least the early fourth century BC. Additionally, although the evidence is far from conclusive, there have also been some archaeological discoveries which may support the presence of clan-based military forces.

As Bietti Sestieri noted in her excavations of Osteria dell'Ossa, in the archaeological record for the early Iron Age in Latium, clans or clan-like social structures/hierarchies are visible in the distribution of graves. Generally, at this site and others, the closer one gets to the centre of these groupings, the wealthier the grave goods and, when one gets right to the centre, there is often a high number of male graves with weapons and other military items.[12] Scholars have interpreted this evidence that there is a strong link between clans, and specifically elite male members of clans, and warfare. This is nothing altogether new, as even in the more traditional models of Roman society there is often a link between the aristocracy and military activity, although the very personal nature of the deposition in a mortuary context and clan grouping suggests that this military identity existed outside of a community structure. Additionally, there have been other finds, like the 125 Negau-style helmets found near Vetulonia in Etruria which were all inscribed with the *gens* name 'Haspnas'. The interpretation of this collection of helmets is still debated, although all of the interpretations still seem to indicate a close connection between *gentes* and war (albeit Etruscan *gentes* from a different region in this instance). It is possible that the helmets represent spoils of war or a trophy of some sort, with the clan inscription being added as part of a dedication. However, it is also possible that they represent part of a store of armour and weapons which were utilized by a *gens* – effectively a family armoury. Given that even the city of Rome did not provide arms and armour for its soldiers until the late Republic, the possible existence of clan-based armouries is intriguing to say the least and may hint at a more sophisticated military structure, which had the possibility of equipping and integrating men who were not usually warriors into the warband/army.

Clan Warfare

The specific implications of the style of warfare in Rome which originated with, and seems to have utilized, warlords and warbands will be discussed in detail in the following chapters, but it is worthwhile to make a few general observations about them here. Perhaps the most important impact of this revised military model is that increasingly early 'Roman' warfare must be understood to have existed as part of a clan-based context and might not be as 'Roman' as usually thought. Although it is likely that the specific benefits and aims of warfare changed significantly based on who was fighting, the basic structure of the armies, their equipment, tactics and approach were likely dictated by the prevalent clan-based model. The implications of this are substantial, particularly when viewed in contrast to a state-based system. For instance, clans seem to have had a much more hierarchical structure than the urban communities of Latium, which likely also resulted in a much more hierarchical military model. Additionally, it is likely that the behaviour and relationships within the early armies may have tended toward clan-based norms, with the general taking on the characteristics of a *paterfamilias*, or clan/family leader, instead of the more limited power of a magistrate or elected official in a civic context. This origin in a clan-based system may help to explain the very different laws and norms which seem to have governed Roman generals and armies while on campaign, even in the late Republic, and particularly the power of 'life or death' which a general had over soldiers under his command. This type of power, which could be invoked without a trial, would represent something of an anomaly in a civic context but represented the norm within Roman clans and was part of the recognized power of a *paterfamilias*.

In a related matter, the clan structure may have also provided the basic mechanism for recruitment. At the core of the clan-based armies was naturally the kinship group, connected by blood and marriage. This group naturally varied in size, but even in the largest clans it would have been limited. As discussed above, it is likely that clans were able to expand the size of their military forces by bringing in outsiders through *sodal* bonds (i.e. sword brothers) or *clientes* (clients). The literary sources indicate that followers and clients followed clans around as they moved, with the Claudii being perhaps the clearest example, and this likely formed a key part of their military forces as well. Although one would not want to push the argument too far, it is possible that this type of patron–client relationship may have also underpinned the soldier–general relationship in more community-based forces. Although it likely did not have the same strength and longevity as more regular patron–client bonds, this type of model for the relationship would also help to explain the types of behaviour and obligations which the sources describe in military contexts. For instance, throughout Roman history there seems to be a very strong set of personal obligations between a general and his soldiers, regarding service and distribution of spoils and wealth, which do not fit within the a legal/civilian framework of a citizen and his elected magistrate. This relationship once again leads us back to the thorny issue of *imperium* and how the clans related to the state through both the *rex* and the later praetors/consuls.

As hinted at in the previous chapter, a detailed discussion of Archaic *imperium* would take up an entire volume in its own right and so is not appropriate here. It is worthwhile to reiterate, however, that *imperium* seems to have had a contractual aspect to it, between the community and the war leader, and to note that the powers included within the grant of *imperium* – including summary execution – seem much more at home within a family or clan model than in a civic context. There are probably some practical considerations present here as well, and one could argue that these powers were derived from a need to keep order within an army and similar powers are present within many other military systems. However, given the existence of the clan model in Rome, and Latium more generally, which already contained these types of powers and relationships, one does not have to search too far or argue that the Romans 'reinvented the wheel' when it came to *imperium*. Rather, they likely drew upon this existing model, or perhaps integrated with it, when developing their armed forces.

Conclusions

The importance of the clan model for warfare in Archaic Central Italy and Rome cannot be overstated. Clans seem to have been the most active military entities in Central Italy during the early Iron Age and both the literary sources and archaeology suggest that the region's communities were relatively late in entering the military game, and indeed only gradually did so with both clans and communities active in military matters, often side-by-side, down into the fourth century BC. The pre-existence, dominance and ultimately persistence of clan warfare in the region shaped the norms, relationships and expectations of warfare in Rome. Armies were hierarchical structures where a variation of clan-based law seems to have predominated and where the general, or warlord, effectively acted as a *paterfamilias*, with all that that entailed. Warfare, as we will see in the following chapters, was also often conducted for aims and goals which might seem more at home in a clan-based setting, with raiding and a pursuit of portable wealth being key. Clans also continued to represent the most active, best equipped and most experienced military entities in the region and as such seem to have formed the core of early state-based forces, giving them a distinct flavour and character. In other words, when the early Romans thought of 'armies', it is likely that their first thought was not of ordered lines of citizen farmers equipped in a uniform fashion and commanded by an elected official, but rather a group of clansmen led by a clan leader. This should also be our default position. Rome's citizen armies which conquered the Mediterranean in the late third and second centuries BC were still centuries away and ultimately emerged because of a very special set of circumstances – indeed this type of army might be considered Hannibal's true legacy in Rome. Rome's army in the late Regal period and early Republic was a very different animal and most likely looked more like an enlarged or expanded clan-based force than a citizen militia – although the seeds of this later army were there.

Chapter 3

The Army in the Fifth Century

The fifth century BC was a tumultuous time for Rome. The century began with Rome still struggling to transition from the period of monarchy and lurching its way, haphazardly, towards the form of government which would eventually be called simply the *res publica* or 'public thing'. The early fifth century BC also saw the beginning of the so-called 'Struggle of the Orders', the perceived conflict between the plebeians and patricians in Rome, which the literary sources present as the backdrop for almost all of the major events and developments in the city during the subsequent 200 years. The 450s BC saw the creation of a law code in Rome, the 'Laws of the Twelve Tables', while the 440s BC witnessed the creation of new magistracies, like the quaestorship and censorship and what may have been an entirely new form of military structure in the 'consular tribunes' (or, alternatively, 'military tribunes with consular power'). The end of the fifth century BC was then taken up with the great conflict with, and ultimate victory over, Veii – although these gains were quickly destroyed by the Gallic sack of Rome c. 390 BC. Nearly all of these events occurred against a backdrop of almost constant warfare with the Etruscans, increasingly bellicose mountain tribes and other Latin peoples.

For the purposes of this book, the military and political developments of the fifth century BC are the most pertinent and arguably the most obvious developments for this period, but they should always be understood as part of a much wider set of changes in Rome and Latium. The incursions of various mountain tribes up and down the peninsula of Italy into the fertile lowland regions, particularly in the west, put increasing military pressure on communities like Rome, Satricum and the Greek communities of Magna Graecia. But this pressure, coupled with some developments in food production, also led to an increase in agricultural investment and production as the communities were forced to maximise the output from increasingly limited sections of land. The fifth century BC was therefore a time of experimentation in Rome – socially, politically, economically and militarily – as the community changed and adapted to larger regional shifts. Most notably, Rome's economic changes and her increased focus on agriculture in the fifth century BC, combined with a decline in foreign trade and trade goods, seems to have slowly changed the goals of warfare, with an ever-increasing focus on land and territorial expansion. The social changes brought about by this mini-agricultural revolution, with an increasingly sedentary and stable population, had a profound impact on the character and identity of Latium's clans and brought their interests more in line with the region's communities.

From Monarchy to Republic

Although it formed a vital aspect of Rome's foundation cycle, and was in all likelihood a pivotal event, Rome's transition from a monarchy to a republic is still largely misunderstood – and again, the fault lies first with the Romans and the nature of the historical tradition. As with most other aspects of their early history, and as already discussed, when the Romans of the late Republic sat down in the late third and second centuries BC to try and decipher where they came from and how their city had developed, they relied heavily on the existing models from the Greek world. Looking at Athens in particular, the Romans saw the removal of the tyrant Hippias *c.* 500 BC, an event which ushered in the Classical period and the rise of a democratic Athens as a major player in Mediterranean politics and society. Looking back at their own muddled oral history, the Romans detected some similarities – most notably the removal of the final Roman *rex c.* 500 BC, the transition to a new form of government and the city's (eventual) rise to power – and so mapped many aspects of Greek history onto her own in order to 'fill in the gaps' and give structure to the city's origins. As a result, the transition from the monarchy to the Republic was perceived by the Romans of the late Republic (and by many modern scholars) as being very similar to the transition from tyranny to democracy in Classical Athens. It supposedly marked a return of power to 'the people' and the advent of a perfectly balanced form of government, combining democracy, oligarchy and monarchy in equal measures, which was praised by Polybius in the second century BC: 'Such being the power that each part has of hampering the others or co-operating with them, their union is adequate to all emergencies, so that it is impossible to find a better political system than this.'[1]

Looking carefully at the literature, however, it is clear that Roman historians were either unable or unwilling to completely hide the real events of the early city under the adopted Greek façade. Most notably, the power of the Roman *reges*, embodied in the grant of *imperium* by the *comitia cruiata* which formed the core of their power, was maintained under the new Republic, as were all of the accoutrements of the office. Some powers were evidently distributed, most notably the sacral elements into the office of the *rex sacrorum*, and the new holders of *imperium* were elected annually and did not hold the office for life, but the core power seems to have remained the same, and was even distributed by the same assembly. Despite the immense amount of emphasis which is traditionally placed on the year 509 BC and the official start of the Republic, the moment did not change things significantly for the majority of people living in Rome. The *comitia curiata* remained the primary (and possibly only) assembly of the people, which still passed the *lex curiata de imperio* which governed the *imperium* of the magistrates. *Imperium* itself also seems to have largely remained the same. The only people who really benefited from this change in government were the powerful elite, who now had a regular opportunity for political advancement within the community – a chance to wield *imperium* and command Rome's military forces. The transition from monarchy to Republic in Rome therefore represented an aristocratic coup, carried out by members of the elite who were evidently close to the *rex*, and was more in response to the growing tension of the increasingly settled aristocratic population in Rome than because of the excesses and arrogance of Rome's leaders. The basic events of the overthrow, which the sources unanimously attest, show a group of aristocrats from outside of Rome (led by Brutus and coming from the nearby community of Collatia) marching on the city and laying out a new system of government which benefited them. The population of Rome seems to have been a largely passive witness in the events, although the people did eventually ratify the outcome by granting *imperium* to the new magistrates. But the end of the monarchy was not a democratic uprising by the people as a whole. Instead, it represented a grab for power by the increasingly large number of clans and clan leaders which were settling around Rome during the period, and the resultant form of government reflected this. The men who took up leadership in Rome, likely adopting the simple title *praetor* ('leader') instead of *rex*, were from the same aristocratic population as the previous *reges* and likely desired the same things. The early Republic was therefore a compromise between these powerful clans, and not necessarily with the community – although the same core relationship with the community via the *curiae*, based around *imperium*, seems to have existed.

But although the core power dynamic between the community and the powerful elite given authority in Rome, defined by *imperium*, remained intact, there were some significant repercussions. The regular change in leadership brought about by the annual nature of the new magistracies likely resulted in a more haphazard and constantly evolving collection of policies. While previously the population and the *curiae* could get to know and probably predict the actions of their *rex*, the aims and purpose of the *praetors* changed each year and likely reflected the individual goals and ambitions of these men and their clans. Additionally, while Rome had always attracted attention because of her great size and population (particularly relative to other communities in the region) and key position on the Tiber, with the possibility open for political advancement in Rome, the city seems to have become the focus of elite attention in Latium. This is most likely seen by the immigration of powerful clans, like the Claudii *c.* 500 BC, and also the increasing tensions between the urban population and the aristocracy as a whole. While the relationship with a single *rex* and his clan was likely manageable, having a large group of aristocrats through whom power regularly rotated seems to have required a bit more finesse – and so it is unsurprising that in the 490s BC the Romans elected the first plebeian tribunes whose duty it was to regulate this relationship.

Porsenna and Lake Regillus

The tensions surrounding this change in government were not only felt within the community, as in the following years Rome came under pressure from a number of powerful outsiders who may have tried to take advantage of what was likely perceived as Rome's weakened position. Without a stable *rex* (and associated clan) to protect the city, Rome's military capability would have varied each year depending on the ability of the annually elected magistrates – something which was true even in later years. The first to challenge Rome, following the removal of the *rex*, was Lars Porsenna of Clusium, a powerful war leader from southern Etruria who attacked Rome in the final years of the sixth century BC.

Just about everything to do with the attack of Porsenna on Rome has been debated, from his intentions to whether he won or lost and the long-term ramifications of the war. The literary sources present a highly mythologized account of his attack which features the heroic stand of Horatius on the bridge across the Tiber, the attempted espionage of Muscius Scaevola and the signing of a peace accord with the Romans after supposedly being impressed by their courage and resistance, although it included the taking of a number of hostages including the famous Cloelia, who escaped Porsenna by swimming across the Tiber.

Given the problematic nature of the account and the highly dramatic character of the various facets, scholars have rightfully been wary of taking any of this narrative at face value. For instance, the sources seem to imply that Porsenna wished to conquer Rome, although there are also suggestions that portable wealth, and particularly cattle, were his main objective – something which would make sense given the existing style of warfare prevalent in the region. A number of scholars have interpreted the peace treaty which concluded the siege as a declaration of surrender by Rome, which was placed in a more favourable light by later historians attempting to erase this ignominious defeat. Indeed, Alfoldi and Howarth both argued that following the treaty, Rome actually fell under the power of Porsenna.[2] One point seems to be clear in this morass, however, and that is that Rome faced a serious threat from a powerful warlord in the final years of the sixth century BC – indeed, a far greater threat than she ever seems to have faced before – and, given that it occurred the year after, in 508 BC, it is likely that it related to the removal of the *rex* in some way.

Supporting this interpretation is the fact that Lars Porsenna was evidently not the only power who felt that Rome was ripe for the taking in the years following the removal of Lucius Tarquinius Superbus, as the city also seems to have come under pressure from both the Etruscans and the Latins during this period, with events coming to a head at the Battle of Lake Regillus in 499 or 496 BC. The Romans evidently won this battle, despite the size of the army arrayed against them, and were able to negotiate a treaty with the rest of the Latins known as the *Foedus Cassianum* (the 'Treaty of Cassius', named after the consul of 493 BC Spurius Cassius Viscellinus). Again though, despite its importance, the details of the battle and its aftermath are both complex and contested. Although the sources are reasonably consistent in claiming the battle was against 'the Latins', and indeed this battle forms the climax of the so-called 'First Latin War', there is still some serious debate over who exactly 'the Latins' were and why they attacked Rome. Both Livy and

Dionysius claim that Tarquinius Superbus was there and had instigated the war, although even Dionysius seems to question the presence of Rome's arch nemesis as he notes that he would have been approaching 90 years old. Indeed, the fact that the Tarquins were associated in some way with every attack on Rome during this period, from that by Porsenna to the Etruscans and the Latins, hints that this may have been something of a literary trope. As for who 'the Latins' were, the common interpretation is that they represented the members of the Latin League – a loose federation of tribes and communities in Latium which met on an annual basis at the *Lucus Ferentinae* to decide on various matters and declare war on common enemies. Unfortunately, most of our information about the league comes from the fourth century BC, when Rome was fully in her ascendency, and indeed the league itself was effectively dissolved after 338 BC with Rome's final conquest of the region. The picture we have then is of a league dominated by Rome, although this domination did not stop the league from attacking Rome during the 340s BC. But the scant evidence we have for the early history of the Latin League is intriguing. Despite their cultural unity and evident association with the geographic region of Latium, the members of the Latin League seem to have had no qualms attacking other Latins and indeed other members of the league (a behaviour which the *Foedus Cassianum* evidently attempted to curtail).

The relative strength of Rome in this period is hard to determine. Although Rome was supposedly in a weakened position in the 490s BC, after the attack of Porsenna and a series of famines and civil unrest, the city was still evidently able to defeat the Latin League's forces. This either indicates that Rome's army, even in the early years of the fifth century BC, represented such a powerful body that it could defeat the combined forces of the rest of the region (not to mention the personal forces of the Tarquins), or that 'the Latins' defeated at Lake Regillus did not represent the full forces of the league. Given the inconclusive warfare which Rome engaged in for the rest of the fifth century BC against individual Latin communities, which will be discussed in the following section, it is highly likely that the latter option is the correct one. If so, this suggests two things which it would be worthwhile to bear in mind when looking at the rest of early Roman warfare. First, one must be very careful when interpreting terms like 'the Latins'. While it is clear that Livy and Dionysius were suggesting that the forces arrayed against Rome represented the full forces of the Latin League, this was likely done for narrative impact more than anything else, and should give us cause to question any other easy, 'catchall' descriptions in the sources for the period (i.e. 'the Etruscans'). Second, it suggests that the military forces of the Latin League were likely an *ad hoc* and haphazard group which may have consisted of different numbers, and indeed different members, each year. This type of unorganised model might also be applied to Central Italy more generally, as evidence suggests that membership in the league, and even among the *Prisci Latini* (Old Latins) who formed the core of the Latin League, seems to have changed depending on which list one looked at. So 'the Latins' which the Romans faced at Lake Regillus may have been any combination of people from Latium, and possibly even outside of the region, although it is likely that they were unified under the auspices and command of the league.

A Century of Inclusive Warfare

Again, perhaps the biggest clue that the Romans did not face off against the full strength of the Latin League in the Battle at Lake Regillus is the inconclusive and indecisive nature of Roman warfare against various individual Latin (and other) opponents during the rest of the fifth century BC. The logic runs that if Rome was able to defeat *all* of the Latins in a single battle, she should have been able to defeat each individual Latin community easily. Although archaeology clearly indicates that Rome was the largest and probably the wealthiest community in Latium during this period, the literary sources suggest that her military forces were incredibly ineffectual during this period

– at least from a late Republican perspective. Although the sources record that the Romans were almost constantly at war during the fifth century BC against a variety of opponents – including the Etruscans, other Latins and invading tribes from the mountainous interior of Italy like the Aequi and the Volsci – the Romans expanded their territory only marginally during the period, with the most significant gain being against the Hernici in the 480s BC. But against the vast majority of her opponents the Romans were often argued to have only been able to achieve something of a stalemate, possibly (following the insinuations of Livy and Dionysius) because of the intensive internal strife caused by the 'Struggle of the Orders'. This conflict between the plebeians and patricians in Rome over access to power, and particularly the highest offices in the city, was often thought to have weakened Rome's military potential and the plebeians are frequently described as boycotting levies and obstructing public business via the actions of the tribunes of the plebs. However, in recent years some scholars are moving away from this interpretation, despite it being supported by the explicit testimony of the literary sources, as it does not explain all of the evidence. Instead of being caused by internal political strife, Rome's inability to expand militarily during the fifth century BC may have simply been a result of the type of warfare being practised.

It may be worthwhile to reiterate here that in the short term at least, despite Rome's transition from a monarchy to a Republic, very little seems to have changed at the top of Rome's political system. The men filling Rome's new annual magistracies came from roughly the same socio-political and economic group as her previous *reges*, and their aims and goals were likely quite similar as well – although their limited term in office may have accelerated their plans. As a result, Rome's early consuls/*praetors*, who represented the powerful clans or *gentes* who still dominated the region (and particularly the extramural regions), probably had their own and their clan's interests firmly at heart when deciding on policies and actions, particularly in the realm of warfare.

As a result, instead of trying to conquer territory which would benefit the community as a whole, these men continued the long-established practice of raiding for portable wealth and booty which would allow them to increase their own wealth and standing. After all, why would one want to spend an entire year campaigning in order to gain control of land which might immediately fall under the power of your political rival the following year? Indeed, it is still entirely uncertain how strong the bond was between any of these powerful war leaders and Rome, despite their holding the consulship. Our late Republican sources naturally assumed that Roman citizenship existed in the early Republic in roughly the same form as it did in the late Republic, and that Rome's elite were all competing against each other to achieve the highest office in Rome as an end in itself – a 'game' which was first explained in the early twentieth century by the great Matthias Gelzer in his examination of the so-called 'Roman Nobility'. But as Gelzer's contemporary, the Italian scholar Gaetano DeSanctis, noted, the consular *fasti* (the list of Rome's magistrates) for this period revealed that the elite seemed to be a much more fluid group than one might expect, with various families regularly appearing and then disappearing from the *fasti*. While it is possible that this type of variation was the result of the problematic transmission of the evidence, DeSanctis argued (and most have since agreed) that this was actually the result of Rome's elite developing over the first half of the fifth century BC as various clans arrived and left Rome, with Rome's aristocracy only solidifying into an identifiable and exclusive group in the late fifth century BC – a point now known as the 'closing of the patriciate'. This fluidity of Rome's aristocracy in the early fifth century BC causes problems for many areas of scholarship, most notably the concept of citizenship, the identity of 'the patricians' and 'the plebeians', the composition of the senate, etc., but it also creates problems for any interpretation of Roman warfare which involves conquest. Why would a fluid aristocracy, which seems to have had only a loose connection to Rome, devote their one year in office in Rome to advancing the aims of the community? If the nature of the office allowed it (and everything we have concerning early *imperium* suggests it did), wouldn't these men have used the system to pursue more personal goals? Looking carefully at the evidence for warfare during this period, the answer is probably 'yes'.

Taking the example of Fidenae, another powerful community located further up the Tiber River and on an important trade route between Latium and Etruria, the community was supposedly founded as a colony by Rome sometime before 500 BC. However, by the 430s BC it was evidently free from any sort of Roman control or domination (if any had actually existed) and represented a rival and important strategic interest in Rome's larger competition with Veii. Roman forces therefore attacked and took the community in 435 BC, but were forced to return less than ten years later and reconquer the site in 426 BC.[3] This type of 'reconquest' is not unique, and similar events can be seen in Rome's interaction with the communities of Crustumerium, Bolae and others. Although the narrative of warfare in Livy and Dionysius clearly depicts wars of conquest followed by occupation and colonization – a system which would have been the norm in a late Republican and early Imperial context – Rome's conquests during this period did not seem to 'stick'. Instead, the Romans were forced to return in only a few years, sometimes more than once, to re-secure the area. So either the Romans were very bad at conquering territory, or there was something else afoot – and hinting at the latter option is Rome's behaviour at Bolae in the final years of the fifth century BC. The community of Bolae was captured by the Romans in 415 BC, although they were forced to return again the next year to capture it again. Neither capture resulted in the foundation of a colony, although both resulted in plunder. Indeed, the second victory was marred by disagreements as it seems that the community had not had enough time to fully recover and so booty for the troops was hard to find. Even in the late fifth century BC, raiding for portable booty seems to have been a major feature of Roman warfare.

A continued focus on raiding, coupled with a slowly coalescing but still heterogeneous and independent elite dominating Rome's military commands, represents the best explanation for the odd character of Roman warfare during the fifth century BC. Rome's early consuls/*praetors* seem to have had their own personal and clan interests at heart for the year they were in charge, and continued to fight and raid much as they had before. The only real difference was that in their year in office they seem to have had access to the manpower of the community to bolster their forces and were likely required to defend the community if needed. So the reason why Rome's warfare at this time seems ineffectual or hard to explain by late Republican standards, is largely because it was not all that 'Roman' in the first place. Instead of being focused on advancing the interests of the community or expanding the territory of Rome, it was instead based around the short-term exploitation of Rome's manpower and resources by the elite elected each year for their own personal benefit and gain. Roman warfare, at least offensively, seems to have represented an extension of clan-based warfare.

Defensively, however, the situation may have been slightly different. While Rome's offensive wars were often boycotted and produced limited results, whenever Rome was attacked the city seems to have mobilized quickly and effectively and was almost universally successful in its defence. Despite Rome engaging in almost constant warfare during the course of the fifth century BC, during that 100-year period the city was never directly attacked or came close to being taken. Instead, as the sources describe time and again, whenever a true threat to the city arose the populace cast aside any political or social disagreements and joined forces in defence of the community and her lands. This unity, and resultant effectiveness in defence was probably the result of a number of factors, but particularly an increasingly shared interest in protecting the city's land. In the sixth century BC and before, many of Rome's elite clans seem to have had only a passing connection to Rome. With most of their wealth in livestock or trade goods, the powerful aristocratic clans could either move their wealth from the city or simply leave the area altogether if put under threat. For instance, when Lars Porsenna attacked in the late sixth century BC, the sources record that this is exactly what many of the populace did – bring the herds inside the community. However, during the course of the fifth century BC more and more of the elite started to settle down permanently in Rome and invested increasingly in agriculture and farmland outside of the city – developments which are increasingly being supported by archaeological survey data from the region. Clearly this had ramifications for a number of aspects of Roman society, but a key impact in the military sphere was that it tied the clans to the city in the long term and gave them all a shared interest in protecting the city's hinterland. As a result, while the various clans, clan leaders and indeed the bulk of the populace might have had reservations about raids or the offensive actions of the city's leaders, they were all unified in defence of their homes, businesses and the farms where the bulk of the city's wealth was increasingly located.

Reforms of the Mid-Fifth Century BC

The first half of the fifth century BC was defined by growing tensions between the population of Rome and the city's increasingly settled clan-based elements. While the clan-based aristocracy, made up of families like the Fabii and the Claudii, monopolized the preatorship and continued to utilize its *imperium* as the *reges* had before, the community as a whole seems to have experienced something of an awakening. Perhaps it was the annual assertion of their political power, through the regular granting of *imperium* to the magistrates, or maybe the continued growth of the city or the increasingly aligned military goals focused on the acquisition and protection of land, but the sources indicate that there was tension in the city. The framework for the tension is often given as a struggle between the patricians and the plebeians – two groups which were present in the late Republic and which were based on roughly hereditary connections. Although the exact origins of both groups are still unclear, and indeed this is still heavily debated, the traditional definitions are usually that the patricians represented the social, political and economic elite in Rome, while the plebeians represented the poorer and generally disenfranchised classes. The patricians supplied the *patres* (fathers) of the early senate and monopolized the magistracies. The plebs represented everyone else. Although by the late Republic there were naturally very wealthy and powerful plebeian families in Rome, for instance the famous *triumvir* Marcus Licinius Crassus or the seven-time consul Gaius Marius, their families were often seen as somehow inferior to the patrician *gentes*. Even in this much later period, the patricians monopolized some of the priesthoods in Rome and still dominated the political scene.

It is unlikely that the patricians and plebeians existed in the fifth century BC in the same form that they did in the late Republic. In the late Republic, these two groups were defined by being first and foremost 'Roman', indeed they represented the two halves of the Roman populace. But given the flexible nature of Roman identity during the sixth and fifth centuries BC, this type of dichotomy is unlikely to have held true in this period, and various alternative models have been put forward. For instance, some scholars in the early twentieth century made the suggestion that the two groups initially represented two distinct ethnic groups, based in part on the hereditary nature of the groups (coupled with some very bad science). Other scholars have argued that the plebeians represented a segment of the Roman population which was disenfranchised by the start of the Republic and formed a separate 'state within a state' in the 490s BC. Yet others have claimed that the entire narrative is largely a late Republican fabrication used to explain some of the more problematic aspects of the historical tradition and to frame events in terms which would make sense in Rome's late Republican political environment. A consensus has yet to be reached on the matter, but a few key points can be drawn out. First, given the events of the middle of the fifth century BC, and particularly the major legal and political changes which occurred, there does seem to have been some sort of internal tension in Rome during this period. Second, given the importance of families and clans in Archaic Central Italy, it is likely that this tension did involve groups which were, at least in part, defined by roughly hereditary links. Third, this tension should probably be seen in the light of the other major developments occurring in Rome during this period, and specifically the gradual settling down of the region's clans in and around Rome. The ultimate conclusion which can be reached from this is that the early stages of the 'Struggle of the Orders' may have reflected the growing tension between the community and the elite clans which had stepped into the void left by the *rex*. Although the community continued to grant the elites power, via *imperium*, the nuances of the relationship, particularly when the clans were not in power, seem to have required some ironing out. Additionally, with the growth of the city and with more and more families being able to compete for leadership within it, the nature of military command and the army itself seems to have evolved. While previously the Roman army of the *rex* and early *praetors* may have resembled an expanded clan army, with the leaders using *imperium* to effectively bring the local population into their clan on a temporary basis, by the middle of the fifth century BC, Rome's population contained quite a few powerful clans in addition to a substantial number of smaller families and unattached individuals. The presence of so many groups and variables seems to have created issues for the Romans, particularly with regards to inclusion and the power dynamics within the community, which resulted in a series of measures which attempted to confront the problem.

The 'Laws of the Twelve Tables' represent one of the first steps in relieving this growing tension in Rome and regulating the various relationships within the burgeoning city. Supposedly created by two sets of *decemviri* (boards of ten men) in 451 and 450 BC, with the first board creating ten tables of the laws and the second an additional two (while also revising some of the earlier tables), the laws were reportedly brought about in response to plebeian demands for concessions from the ruling elite. From the remains of the law code which has been preserved in our sources, the majority of the laws seem to have been concerned with regularizing and formalizing basic relationships (including the patron–client bond), laying out fines and establishing a sense of order. For proponents of the traditional model and narrative of Roman development, this rather mundane character of the law code has caused some consternation. After all, would the Romans need a new law code to lay out these basic rules if they were already a cohesive society with a strong state structure? However, if one accepts that Rome's society was both a fluid and rapidly growing one, where a significant proportion of the urban population may have been feeling increasingly bullied by the newly arrived clans who had made the city their home, this type of law code starts to make a bit more sense. Although it does not necessarily offer concessions to the plebeians, or indeed any other segments of Roman society, it does establish a base set of rules which should be followed within the confines of the city; a set of rules which could be seen and must be accepted by all, including the city's newcomers and most notably the region's clans who had previously relied on a more patriarchal form of law determined by the *paterfamilias* (family head).

Rome's next major developments occurred only a few years after and were, again, largely administrative in nature. Specifically, Rome created several new offices tasked with regulating the burgeoning city and dealing with interconnecting sets of needs. The first was the office of the quaestorship, or specifically the *quaestores aerarii*, who were created in 447 BC and tasked with overseeing the financial aspects of the state and an increasing number of other administrative duties. According to tradition, these quaestors were not the first in Rome, as during the Regal period the *reges* supposedly appointed, on an *ad hoc* basis, *quaestores parricidii* to help in legal matters and particularly prosecuting murders – the term quaestor coming from the Latin word *quaerere*, meaning 'to seek' or 'investigate'.

The evidence for these early officials is ambiguous at best, as they represented minor magistrates tasked with the more mundane aspects of civic management so did not appeal to historians looking for 'great men' performing 'great deeds'. But the decision to create a permanent set of magistrates in charge of running the day-to-day aspects of city life was in fact an important one, as it suggests that Rome had reached a size and sophistication to require such an office. The quaestorship, in effect, represented the birth of the Roman bureaucracy, the very existence of which indicates a level of self-awareness which arguably did not exist previously.

While these changes were important, the years 444 and 443 BC were momentous as they witnessed the advent of the censorship and the consular tribunes – two new offices which should be viewed and understood together. Beginning with the censorship, this magistracy was tasked with defining the Roman populace. They conducted the census, which counted the citizens in Rome and placed them into their appropriate groups, and were in charge of the rites associated with the *lustrum*, which represented a purification of the people and a ritual delineation of the city's boundaries. The office also represents the first magistracy which was elected via the *Comitia Centuriata* (Centuriate Assembly), and was inexorably connected with that body – as the censor was in charge of determining where each citizen fitted into the system of classes and centuries. As a result, although the sources claim that the census conducted by the first censors was actually the seventh in the history of the city (the earlier incarnations being done by the *reges* or consuls/*praetors*), it has been plausibly suggested that this period, and not the reign of Servius Tullius a hundred years previously, represents the more logical time for the advent of the Centuriate reforms. The existence of a permanent magistracy associated with the census is also an interesting development. Famously, there are generally two reasons for a census: taxation and war. Given that the Romans did not seem to adopt any form of formal taxation for several more decades, the military motivation for the creation of the censorship logically comes to the fore. This is why scholars have always been curious about the creation of a new military office which coincides with the advent of the censorship, the office of the consular tribunate.

The consular tribunes, or military tribunes with consular power (*tribuni militum consulari potestate*), are some of the most enigmatic figures from early Roman history. While the vast majority of Rome's other republican magistracies continued into the more historical period of the late Republic in a form which at least vaguely seemed to resemble their earlier incarnation, the consular tribunes represent something of an anomaly. First, it should be noted that the title of the early office is still not actually known. Livy usually describes the magistrates as *tribuni militum consulari potestate*, but other variations also exist. For instance, Livy also refers to them as *tribuni militum pro consulibus*, a variation which was also picked up by Aulus Gellius (Gell. *NA* 14.7, Liv. 4.7), although Gellius used the version *tribuni militum consulari imperio* as well (Gell. *NA* 17.21). Despite the variation, it can be argued that the officials were likely known as *tribuni militum*, although not of the standard variety. Now anyone familiar with Rome's late Republican army will recognize the title of military tribune, or tribune of the soldiers, as these men represented the primary officer class in the later army. Made up of young men, typically in their twenties, they were elected every year and assigned to Rome's various armies. So in the late Republic the military tribunes represented low ranking officers whose office was effectively a stepping stone before starting properly on the *cursus honorum* (the sequence of Roman political offices). The military tribunes with consular power, however, seem to have represented the very top of Rome's political order when they were created and, apart from the obvious military associations, did not seem to share any attributes with the later officials of the same name. Additionally, to make matters more complicated, there are references in the sources to regular (i.e. of the late Republican variety) military tribunes also in existence during the fifth century BC. So in many ways, the title of military tribune with consular power raises more questions than it answers when trying to determine the nature of the office.

A second mystery which surrounds the magistracy is its short-lived and fluid nature. The office was introduced in 444 BC, supposedly in response to plebeian clamouring for reform, but then disappeared in 376 BC, also in response to plebeian pressure, and was ultimately replaced by a revamped consulship in 367 BC. As a result, while the Romans knew that this office had once existed, based on evidence from the *fasti*, sources like the *annales maximi* and possibly the oral tradition, they would have had only the vaguest recollection of what it was and seem to have been rather confused about it themselves. Both Livy and Dionysius offer a range of explanations for the creation of the office in the 440s BC, which feature both political pressures and military necessity as the two basic options. But the narrative itself, for the roughly seventy years of the office's existence, is problematic to say the least. First, the office itself was not stable. The number of consular tribunes elected seems to have changed over time, starting off with three in 444 BC, then moving to four in the 420s BC and ultimately six in the final years of the fifth century BC. Additionally, although the office was supposedly introduced in response to very real and pressing issues, consular tribunes were only elected for roughly half of the years between 440 and 400 BC. In the other years, consuls/*praetors* were elected instead, without a real reason offered as to why or a discernible pattern in the choice. The traditional argument for the decision to go with consuls or consular tribunes, as given by Livy, related to military necessity and suggested that the Romans created the office in part to deal with the increased number of wars she found herself engaged in and therefore opted for consular tribunes when more than two commanders were needed in a given year. However, this argument has been generally refuted by the fact that Rome would have had to make the decision concerning which type of official to elect many months before her military needs were actually known. The political reason offered for the creation of the office, that it represented a way for plebeians to attain the highest office in the city, also fails to pass muster as the office was still monopolized by the patrician elite for the vast majority of its existence – so if it was designed as a mechanism to allow for more patrician-plebeian equality it was an absolute failure.

There are also questions concerning the nature of the power wielded by the tribunes and whether they held *imperium* or not. The argument against is based largely on the fact that not a single consular tribune celebrated a triumph, that ritual which was so intimately associated with *imperium*, during the entire history of the office. While this is not conclusive evidence by any stretch of the imagination, the absence of triumphs for the consular tribunes is significant given the regularity with which they were celebrated by the early consuls/*praetors*. Those who argue that the tribunes did have *imperium* often do so based on the simple argument that they must have as they clearly commanded armies – taking *imperium* as simply the right to command – along with problematic references, like that in Gellius, which refer to the officials as 'military tribunes with consular imperium' (*tribuni militum consulari imperio*). However, as already noted, *imperium* seems to have represented far more than just the ability to command an army, as the myriad rituals and accoutrements associated with the power indicate. Additionally, as has been argued in the previous chapters, the consuls/*praetors* did not have a monopoly on military leadership as every clan leader likely commanded their own private 'army' in clan-based actions on a regular basis; so assuming that it was required for military leadership is problematic. A number of possible solutions have therefore been suggested. Some have suggested that the consular tribunes did wield *imperium*, and so commanded armies in the traditional fashion, but either failed to achieve the requirements for a triumph or were somehow barred from celebrating one. Alternatively, it is possible that the consular tribunes did not wield *imperium*, but commanded armies via a different mechanism. *Imperium* seems to have initially represented a bond between a foreign warlord and the community. But, given the development of the community in terms of size, sophistication and cohesion in the fifth century BC, it may be possible to suggest that the Romans were ready to try and look internally for a military commander, and that the consular tribunes represented their first attempt at this.

The evidence for the consular tribunes representing a new form of military leadership based, first and foremost, on the community is circumstantial but plausible – and arguably represents the most logical explanation for this enigmatic development. The strong association between the consular tribunes and the office of the censorship, as they were created at the same time and quite possibly overlapped in terms of power, hints that both offices were created in response to the same set of social and political conditions. Key amongst these conditions was a reassessment of what it meant to be Roman and therefore what it meant to lead and be part of a Roman army. Although there is no direct evidence for a change in recruitment patterns and practices after the creation of the office, the armies fielded by the consular tribunes did seem to be understood as somehow different. As noted, the armies of the consular tribunes did not celebrate triumphs, but more importantly, after the city was sacked by the Gauls in 390 BC (as will be discussed in the next chapter), Rome suddenly reverted completely to using consular tribunes for the next fourteen years. While previously the office had irregularly alternated with the old praetorship/consulship, and indeed had largely been replaced by the old office in the final years of the fifth century BC, after Rome's great loss to the Gauls the city decided that only consular tribunes should be selected, presumably as they were the best suited to defend the city. The consular tribunes and their armies were therefore understood to be the city's most effective form of defence, were associated with the census (and very likely the new assemblies it was based on) and quite possibly did not wield *imperium* (which is generally associated with warlords from outside the community) – all hinting at a very new form of military leadership which may have been in charge of a new, more inclusive Roman army – indeed, what may be the early Centuriate Army.

The Roman Army of the 5th Century BC

The Roman army of the fifth century BC obviously reflected the social and political changes occurring in Rome, although the development was evidently subtle. From an outsider's perspective, very little would have changed in how the Roman army looked or was equipped from the Regal armies of the sixth century BC to the armies of the early Republic. Although military equipment disappears almost entirely from the archaeological record for the fifth century BC in Latium, what little evidence we do have (most notably the Lanuvium warrior burial, dated to *c.* 500 BC, some problematic sculptures from temple pediments and possible comparative evidence from Etruria) all suggests continuity rather than change. Roman and Latin warriors still seem to have equipped themselves in heavy bronze armour when they could, although there is some evidence for increased use of cheaper variations like the linen cuirass (*linothorax*). There are also gradual developments in helmet type, generally favouring cheaper options, although largely maintaining the previously existing style and function. This continuity makes sense as, for the most part, the soldiers making up the army seem to have been coming from the same groups as before and were likely using inherited equipment – although there are some hints that the pool for soldiers was gradually expanding during this period to include new members of the 'upper middle class' within the community (it is probably these new additions which favoured the cheaper options). The core of the army, however, remained the traditional forces of the *gentes* and they seem to have continued to use predominantly thrusting spears and the occasional sword in combat, which still seems to have been focused largely on individual duelling in close combat.

The real differences in the army, as discussed above, were in organization – although this would ultimately have a significant impact on how the army would have behaved in the field. The gradual transition from a fundamentally gentilicial or clan-based military structure, to one based on the community, seems to have resulted in a certain level of disorder in the ranks – as in the second half of the fifth century BC there are suddenly references to armies acting in a mutinous or disobedient fashion. Although this may represent a later literary embellishment, this type of behaviour does make some sense if the command structure, power dynamic and indeed the ultimate goals and aims of the army were changing – not to mention the inclusion of an increasing number of 'new' troops from the urban community of Rome. No longer were the goals and command structure necessarily aligned along long-standing and traditional clan-based lines, where the word and power of a *paterfamilias* reigned supreme – and again, this seems to have been the case even in Rome's previous armies controlled via *imperium* – but instead everything was passing through the new (and still quite fluid) matrix of the community. Although this new system seems to have resulted in the possibility of slightly larger armies, it did not always result in more effective armies – and particularly not for the powerful, clan-based elite.

Veii and the Etruscans

The capture of the city of Veii represents a key transition point in Rome's military development. Veii was early Rome's primary rival – indeed THE rival – during the Archaic period. But while the sources are unanimous about the presence of regular conflict between the two communities during the course of the fifth century BC, the exact reasons behind it are rather hard to pinpoint. Much has been made of the fact that the two cities represented two different cultures – the Romans being Latin and the Veientines Etruscan – and that the war may have represented a shift in regional power between these two groups. The Etruscans were, and indeed remain, a rather mysterious people – an attribute which they intentionally cultivated as time went on – and their origins represent one of the more public debates in modern scholarship on Archaic Italy. The Etruscans spoke a non-Indo-European language, indicating from the outset that there was something different about this group in Italy. The two contrasting arguments are that they either represented an ancient remnant of some pre-existing society which managed to resist the influence of the Indo-European dialects that spread west from the Caucasus, or they were a later arrival to the area who brought their own language with them. Additionally, Etruscan culture seems to have developed along a rather unique course in Italy – urbanizing before any other areas, engaging in long-distance trade with the east from an early date and containing quite a few eccentricities relating to fashion, art, religion and numerous other aspects of life – which all served to encourage this sense of being 'different'. Indeed, even the Romans seem to have thought that the Etruscans were different and perhaps 'otherworldly'. Well after their culture went into decline, the Etruscans were renowned as soothsayers, as they were thought to have more insight than others into the divine workings of the gods.

The ancient sources record a number of possible origin stories for the Etruscans, many of which saw them as immigrants from the East – possibly from modern-day Turkey. The earliest of these stories can actually be found in the Greek historian Herodotus, writing in the fifth century BC, and various versions were regularly presented by different authors for the next half a millennium and more. This subject has been taken up by a range of modern scholars from various fields – ranging from chemistry, to linguistics and (naturally) history – who have all endeavoured to explain where the Etruscans came from. Some have tried to bolster Herodotus' suggestion of an Asian origin by looking at DNA, while others attempted to link them with the mysterious Sea Peoples or (taking a more fanciful turn) perhaps even the refugees from the lost

Plates

Military equipment finds, and even depictions of warriors, from Rome's regal and early republican periods are incredibly rare. A few pieces of terracotta showing what *may* be warriors – gods, demigods, etc. are also options - is about all we have from the city itself. This has forced scholars to look outside of Rome for evidence. This search obviously includes Latium, but scholars have also looked to the north and Etruria. In Etruria archaeologists have unearthed some significant finds, most notably at sites like Caere/Cerveteri and Tarquinia, although it has always been difficult assess how much of this evidence is applicable to the Roman context given the cultural differences which existed between the regions. It is possible that Roman and Etruscan warriors equipped themselves similarly but, given the problems with interpreting the mortuary deposits (which contain a strong ritual component) and the artwork (which may have been done by foreign artists), even determining how Etruscan warriors may have equipped themselves is problematic – making any parallels to Rome all that much more tenuous. The evidence from Latium, the region which includes Rome and extends further south, is arguably a bit better source of information – although the finds are much more limited. The evidence for military equipment amounts of an odd assortment of minor finds (spear points, etc.) supplemented by few exceptional burials, like the Lanuvium warrior burial shown below, along some architectural terracottas like those shown below from Signia and Satricum. But the archaeological evidence for Roman itself in the archaic period is limited to say the least. Figures 1–3 offer an indicative selection.

Looking a bit later, however, as Rome expanded south into Campania in the 4th century BC, some additional sources of evidence are arguably applicable. Most notably, given the strong connection between Roman warfare and Samnite/Lucanian warfare during the period – seen not only in the literary traditions, but also in the similarities between equipment finds – it may be possible to use the much richer iconographic evidence from this region to provide at least a rough context for Roman military development during this period. Figures 3-9 illustrate these types of finds, which are useful in showing the both the norms and the diversity of warfare in the region and period. Figure 9 in particular, which illustrates a full warrior panoply dating to the 4th century BC found near the site of Paestum (south of the Bay of Naples) is noteworthy for the strong similarities it has to the Lanuvium panoply of a century earlier. Although there are some significant differences in terms of style, particularly for the helmet and cuirass, the types of armour and weaponry are remarkably similar given the differences in time, location, and (supposedly) culture. This suggests that 'elite' warriors, who would have worn this equipment, likely equipped themselves (and fought) in a reasonably consistent manner across Central Italy during these centuries.

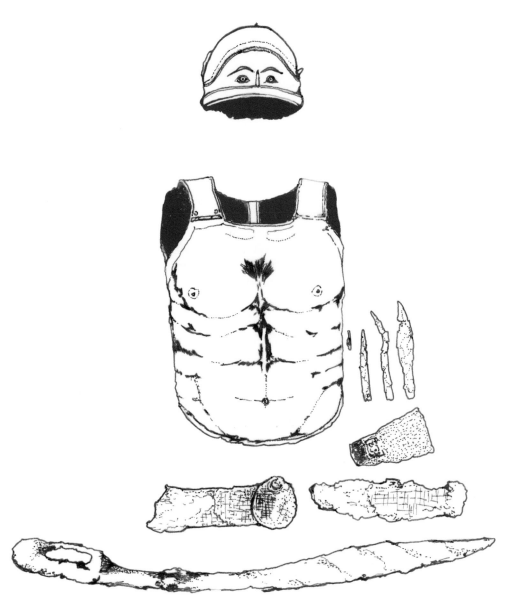

Fig. 1. Drawing of the military equipment finds from the Lanuvium warrior burial, *c.* 500 BC. *Illustration by Katrina Edwards. Reproduced with permission*

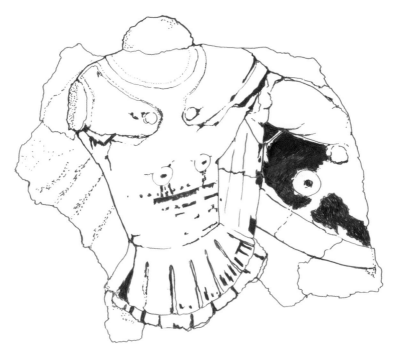

Fig. 2. Drawing of an architectural terracotta from Signia (Temple to Juno Moneta) with the torso of a warrior in a linen cuirass, 5th century BC. *Illustration by Katrina Edwards. Reproduced with permission*

Fig. 3. Drawing of an architectural terracotta from Satricum (Temple to Mater Matuta) with the torso of a warrior in a linen cuirass, 5th century BC. *Illustration by Katrina Edwards. Reproduced with permission*

Fig. 4. Tomb painting depicting a warrior's return (Paestum, Tomba Adriuolo 12 – eastern slab, 375–370 BC). Picture from the National Archaeological Museum of Paestum. *Photo taken by Francesco Valletta and John Grippo. Reproduced with permission*

Fig. 5. Tomb painting depicting a warrior's panoply and a cavalryman (Paestum, Tomba Adriuolo 61 – southern slab, 320–300 BC) Picture from the National Archaeological Museum of Paestum. *Photo taken by Francesco Valletta and John Grippo. Reproduced with permission*

Fig. 6. Tomb painting depicting a battle scene (Paestum, Tomba Adriuolo 114 – northern slab, 330–320 BC) Picture from the National Archaeological Museum of Paestum. *Photo taken by Francesco Valletta and John Grippo. Reproduced with permission*

Fig. 7. Tomb painting depicting a duel (Paestum, Tomba Arcioni 1 – western slab, 375–350 BC) Picture from the National Archaeological Museum of Paestum. *Photo taken by Francesco Valletta and John Grippo. Reproduced with permission*

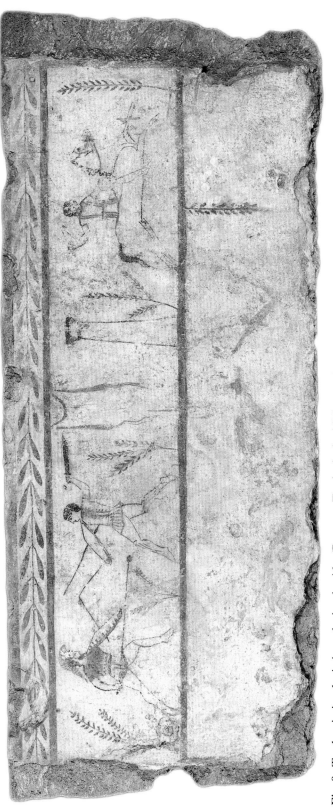

Fig. 8. Tomb painting depicting a duel and a rider (Paestum, Tomba Arcioni 271 – southern slab, 400–375 BC) Picture from the National Archaeological Museum of Paestum. *Photo taken by Francesco Valletta and John Grippo. Reproduced with permission*

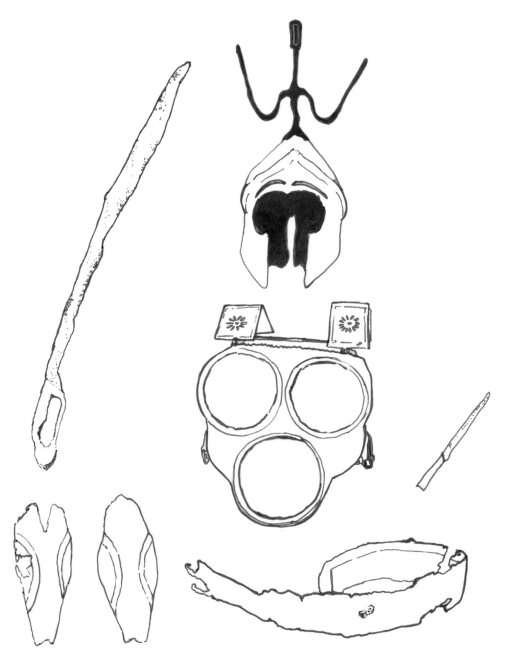

Fig. 9. Drawing of the military equipment finds from the Paestum warrior burial, Tomb 174 Gaudo, 390–380 BC. *Illustration by Katrina Edwards. Reproduced with permission*

continent of Atlantis. But although there is still some public debate about this subject, particularly amongst non-specialists, most archaeologists have settled on a basic narrative based firmly on the surprisingly mundane and simple explanation offered by the archaeology. While the language and certain aspects of Etruscan culture do suggest 'differentness', the vast majority of the archaeology indicates the Etruscans were in fact a native population which developed out of the same Bronze Age culture as the various other Italian groups – indeed the Etruscans and Latins seem to represent branches of the same 'Proto-Villanovan' people which lived in Italy as late as the start of the Iron Age. Looking outside of the more exotic elements of Etruscan society and focusing on basic aspects like burial practices, pottery production and the like, it becomes clear that Etruscan society should be considered part of the same pattern of development as the rest of Italy. The trick is then explaining the various exotic elements, which is usually done by emphasizing the importance of Etruscan trade networks.

The region of Etruria, with its mineral-rich north, fertile south, long coastline and river valleys, offered the Etruscans a perfect location for trade. Exporting raw materials along with some finished goods, the Etruscans were able to grow immensely wealthy during the seventh and sixth centuries BC. Relying on both maritime and land-based routes, the Etruscans largely traded with the new Greek colonies which had been planted in the south of Italy – an area which would soon become known as Magna Graecia. Through this trade the Etruscans were able to bring in a massive range of items from the east; in fact, when archaeologists first began to excavate Etruscan sites in the eighteenth and nineteenth centuries, they found so many Greek pots that they assumed there must have been Greeks living there. This mercantile, and arguably consumerist, culture may help to explain some of the more exotic elements of Etruscan society – these aspects may have come along with the trade and resulted from the simple exposure to many foreign cultures, particularly the Greeks and Phoenicians. It is also possible that the wealth and opportunities present in Etruria encouraged some small groups of migrants to move to the region from the east, which ultimately gave rise to the myth that they had all emigrated from the region. Indeed, the sources suggest that the ancestors of the Tarquins were originally from Corinth, hinting that this narrative may hold true for some at least. It is also possible that that these few migrants brought the characteristic Etruscan language with them. Given that our only knowledge of this language comes from writing, which was something generally associated with trade in its earliest phases, it is possible that it spread from that source and did not, originally, represent the native dialect of the people as a whole.

The Etruscans, therefore, should be considered a powerful trading people, based to the north of Rome, who developed a distinct cultural identity during the seventh and sixth centuries BC, based in part on their exposure to various eastern cultures. However, at their core they were still Italian, as seen in the many aspects of their daily life which mirror those in other Italian cultures. Although they urbanized more quickly than the other Italian peoples, their basic society was still fundamentally based on clans and clan structures, which seem to have been retained even within the urban environments. As a result, scholars have begun to suggest that the Etruscans would not have looked quite as foreign to the early Romans as commonly thought, and in fact it might be hard to tell an Etruscan elite from a Latin or Sabine one. Yes, the Etruscans seem to have had a bit more wealth and perhaps a little more flair and fashion sense, but the perceived cultural divide between the Latins and Etruscans has increasingly been eroded the more we learn about the two groups, particularly amongst the elite. During the Archaic period, the elite from Etruria, Latium and all of Central Italy seem to have moved about so much that they effectively formed their own society. This is arguably why the Romans were able to accept an Etruscan warlord as a *rex* when they took the elder Tarquin, in the same way that they had accepted a Sabine when Numa became *rex* – to the people of Rome, they were all variations on a theme.

Returning to Veii and Rome's conflict with that city, while there may be some kernel of truth in the old narrative of Rome finally ending the domination of the Etruscans with the capture of the city, the underlying narrative is likely to be more economic than cultural. Etruscan power had been based largely on trade with the Greeks in southern Italy. But during the course of the fifth century BC, this trade went into decline because of both the incursions of peoples of the mountainous interior of Italy across the north/south trades which ran the length of the peninsula and increasing conflict between the Etruscans and the Greeks themselves (not to mention the chaotic nature of Greek politics and warfare itself during the second half of the century). Although the Etruscans were clearly very good merchants, they were also renowned as pirates – indeed, in the ancient world the terms were effectively synonymous with the difference between a merchant and pirate being simply opportunity and circumstance. During the fifth century BC, it seems as if the Greeks of southern Italy became increasingly annoyed with continued Etruscan raiding and gradually cut commercial ties with them. All of this led to a gradual decline in Etruria which, when it happened to coincide with an emerging and powerful Rome, ultimately spelled doom for the once proud people. In the mid-fifth century BC, however, things were still very much in flux. Rome was still coalescing and finding its identity as a single community, which contained both the old urban core and its new elite clans, while Veii was still struggling to maintain control of its hinterland, and particularly the trade routes across the Tiber River which linked it to the Greeks in the south. It is likely control of these trade routes that brought Rome into the conflict with Veii, along with the usual aristocratic raiding which went on between the two (and probably formed the core of the famous war in the 470s BC which resulted in the defeat of the Fabii at the Cremera River). Rome's conflict with Veii in the final decades of the fourth century BC can therefore be seen as part of Rome's increasing control of the trade which still ran through the region. The end result of the victory in 396 BC, which supposedly came after a ten-year siege of the city by the Romans, was for Rome to emerge as the main economic powerhouse in the region which effectively controlled all of the north/south land-based trade running through the western half of the Italian peninsula.

As an interesting aside, the siege of Veii also marked the introduction of the *stipendium militum* – or pay for soldiers – which was supposedly introduced in order to keep the army in the field during the decade-long siege of the city. The advent of the *stipendium*, if it can indeed by tied to this period (something which is by no means certain), may indicate some interesting things about how much the Roman army had developed by the turn of the century. First, it indicates that warfare was something which the community wanted to invest in – that victory was something which was good for the entire community. While in the past this would definitely have been true for defensive wars, for offensive wars, like that against Veii, the only real benefits acquired would have been for the soldiers in the army in the form of booty and loot. However, there seems to have been something about the war against Veii which convinced the populace to support it financially. Perhaps it was the monopolization of the trade routes or even the final removal of the city's old rival, but the introduction of the *stipendium* indicates that, arguably for the first time, the community of Rome as a whole was invested, quite literally, in the actions of its army in the field. Also, albeit in a connected point, the *stipendium* hints at a much more strategic approach to warfare. The *stipendium* was supposedly introduced in order to offset the costs of the war for the soldiers involved. In the past, this had been unnecessary as offensive wars were generally quite short and the soldiers were able to offset their costs, and ideally augment their income, through the immediate proceeds (i.e. booty) acquired each year. However, the siege of Veii, whether it lasted the reported ten years or not, seems to have required some patience on the part of the army with regards to its reward – with the *stipendium* being set up to negate that. So in addition to the community investing in the conflict, by 396 BC, the army seems have developed quite a bit – no longer engaging solely in single-year raiding but instead working towards major goals in multi-year campaigns. The Roman army *c.* 400 BC was therefore far less reactionary than the army of 100 years previous, and arguably much more community focused.

Conclusion

The fifth century BC represents one of the most important periods in the development of the Roman army, as the century begins with an army which still acted like an extension of an aristocratic clan but ended with a community-based force, led (at least in some years) by a new type of magistrate, and which was financially backed by the community and able to take on multi-year missions. The fifth century BC also saw the first real movements toward a cohesive community, which included both aristocratic clans and the urban population, which would ultimately form the foundation for this new military force. However, despite all the changes, the Roman army was still very much in its infancy and there seems to have been the possibility that things would revert to the old aristocratic way of doing things. Despite the evident potential of Rome's new community-based army, it seems as if many of the elite had yet to be won over to this new way of doing things. In many years, and increasingly commonly *c.* 400 BC, the Roman state went back to selecting consuls/ *praetors* instead of consular tribunes, in spite of the military benefits which the consular tribunes seem to have had. Although the reasons behind this choice are impossible to determine, it is likely that they were connected to the new community focus of the revamped army, as this did not suit everyone's needs. The new army was effective and seems to have represented something which the community could support and rally behind. However, this community focus may have also dictated the aims and goals of the army toward more community-centred objectives and away from the traditional goals of acquiring wealth and prestige for the leaders. This is perhaps best exemplified by the fact that the consular tribunes did not celebrate triumphs – which were intensely personal celebrations of victory in war and the acquisition of spoils by a general. The new consular tribunes seem to have gone too far in the community direction to please the elites who were still settling down around the community and who may not have fully bought into the new ethos. In order for that to happen, something significant was needed – something which would force them to recognize that the benefits of participating in a community-based army and style of warfare outweighed the loss of freedom which it entailed. Something like the sack of the city by an army of Gauls.

Chapter 4

The Gallic Sack and Rome's Rebirth

The sack of Rome by the Gauls *c*. 390 BC represented a 'watershed moment' in early Roman history, after which nothing was quite the same.[1] This was the point identified by Livy as the 'second birth' (*secunda origine*) of the city and the moment he selected as the starting point of his second 'pentad' (set of five books) in his history. In other words, if Livy was a Hollywood filmmaker making a series of movies about early Rome, the first installation would have started with Aeneas and Romulus and culminated with the city's victory over Veii, and the second would start with the epic tragedy of the Gallic sack and Rome's rise to greatness in the century following. So, for the Romans, the sack of Rome and the associated defeat at the River Allia clearly represented a turning point in their history – although one whose significance had changed and been adapted over time.

For Livy and the historians of the late Republic, the primary significance of the sack of Rome seems to have been that it marked the point at which evidence seemed to get a bit more reliable. At the start of book 6, Livy famously noted that 'from this point onwards a clearer and more definite account shall be given of the City's civil and military history'.[2] The problematic nature of the evidence for the preceding centuries was usually blamed on the destruction of records in a great fire caused by the sack, although there is minimal archaeological evidence to support this.[3] Livy hints at this event though, saying the faulty data for the fifth century BC is in part the result of an *incensa*, although the timing and nature of the fire is disputed with some scholars arguing that it actually refers instead to a second century BC fire at the *regia* – associated with the *pontifex maximus*, where records were stored. For the rest of the Roman populace in the late

Republic, the Gallic sack seems to have marked a time of ill-omen, made famous by the *Dies Alliensis* (*Day of the Allia*), which commemorated the defeat which led to the sack, but probably little more than that – at least after Caesar's conquest of Gaul and the final removal of the great Gallic threat. However, in the context of the period, the importance of the Gallic sack of Rome *c.* 390 BC cannot be overstated. Although it probably did not produce any immediate changes in its own right, despite the assertions of Plutarch and others, it did provide an immense catalyst for change and accelerated the numerous social, political and military developments which were already underway in Rome. Specifically, and focusing on the Roman army, the victory by the Gauls sounded the final death knell for the archaic clan-based warband as the primary military unit in Rome. Although these continued to exist throughout the fourth century BC in various parts of Italy, their ineffectiveness against the Gauls in 390 BC demonstrated quite clearly to the Romans that their time was over. The trauma of the sack also seems to have brought the Roman community together in a way it had never experienced before. While previously the community had represented a slightly amorphous and fluid population based around the urban centre of Rome, the aftermath of the sack witnessed the true advent of a distinct Roman identity – a '*Romanitas*' or 'Roman-ness' – that would develop into the more concrete Roman citizenship, which later Romans would prize so dearly. This new sense of *Romanitas* would go on to drive the social and political developments of the fourth century BC as well, including the end of the 'Struggle of the Orders'. But more importantly for the Roman army during this period, it would allow (or perhaps force) the creation of a new set of military commanders (the consuls), a more strategic approach to military actions based on conquest, a new approach to captured land (citizen colonies) and eventually a new tactical formation (the so-called 'manipular legion'). In this context, the Gallic sack seems to have pushed Rome over the edge of the cliff of social, military and political development she had been walking along up to that point – venturing near it, only to pull back and regress to her archaic *modus operandi*. The arrival of Gauls in serious numbers in the early fourth century BC demonstrated that the Romans would need to adapt or face utter destruction – and so adapt they did.

The Gallic Sack

The sack of Rome by the Gauls was the culmination of a series of battles (and defeats) which are described in some detail by a huge range of authors (Cato, Polybius, Livy, Dionysius of Halicarnassus, Diodorus Siculus, Plutarch, Pliny the Elder, Pompeius Trogus, Appian and others). These battles included an initial skirmish between members of the Fabii clan and the Gauls near the city of Clusium, the major defeat of a combined Roman army at the River Allia and finally the 'siege' and subsequent capture of at least most of the city of Rome itself. There are also some accounts which suggest that there was yet another battle after the sack, which the Romans are supposed to have won, when the Roman general Camillus, who had been recalled from exile during the siege, chased down the Gauls in order to recapture the gold paid as an indemnity. This final (and incredibly dubious) battle aside, the Gallic sack represented a comprehensive defeat of Rome's armed forces which was done without the benefit of surprise or an ambush. The sources are unanimous that Rome's forces were simply outmatched.

Although the details of the events vary quite a bit between the surviving sources, and the archaeological evidence for the sack is (perhaps surprisingly, given its supposed violence) almost non-existent, the capture of the city by the Gauls represents one of the few aspects of early Roman history which even the most suspicious of scholars can feel reasonably confident in. First, and perhaps foremost, the sack of Rome by the Gauls seems to have left an indelible mark on the Roman psyche, and created a longstanding cultural 'bogeyman', inspiring the *metus Gallicus* ('Gallic fear') which even Hannibal and the *metus Punicus* ('Punic/Carthaginian fear') could not top. From this period on, the Gallic menace arguably represented Rome's greatest anxiety – one which was only put to rest by Caesar and his campaigns in Gaul (an oft forgotten aspect of his *Bellum Gallicum*). The date of the defeat at the River Allia was remembered for centuries as a day of ill-omen and the fear of another attack by the Gauls led to the immediate institution of the *tumultus Gallicus*, a mass conscription in defence of the city, and indirectly to the creation of Rome's alliance network in the fourth century BC. The sack of Rome by the Gauls also represents one of the first specific mentions of Rome in the historical record, as it was recorded by Aristotle (preserved in Plutarch's *Life of Camillus*) along with a number of other late fourth century BC Greek writers.[4] This was an event which reverberated even outside of Italy.

Out of the surviving sources for the sack, Livy offers the most complete account and the most detail for the events leading up to it, suggesting both an interest and familiarity with the story which may have resulted from his upbringing in Patavium in Cisalpine Gaul. Livy's account indicates that the history of the Gauls in Italy goes back to the final years of the sixth century BC when a group, under the command of the two nephews of the Gallic chief Ambigatus, ventured out from their homelands in Southern Gaul looking for land. One nephew, Segovesus, took his people into the Hercynian highlands in Southern Germany but the other, Bellovesus, took his followers south across the Alps into Northern Italy. Once there, Livy claimed that Bellovesus and his people destroyed an Etruscan army near the River Ticinus and founded the city of Mediolanium, modern Milan. After a few years, a group of settlers left Mediolanium under the command of Etitovius and settled even further south, near Brixia and Verona. This was followed by still further waves of Gallic settlers who ventured further and further south, with the Libui, Salluvi, Boii, Lingones and Senones all pushing into Etruscan and later Umbrian land – settling in the region which would become Cisalpine Gaul. According to Livy it was then the Senones, the last of the tribes to venture south from Southern Gaul, which made its way to Rome under the leadership of Brennus, before heading even further south to take up service as mercenaries under the tyrant Dionysius I of Syracuse.

Undoubtedly based on local traditions in Cisalpine Gaul, Livy's account meshes well with what we know about the region archaeologically and indirectly from other literary sources. It has long been established that the late sixth and fifth centuries BC were hard times for the Etruscans, as they came under increasing pressure from Gauls from the north along with the decline of trade with the Greek communities of Magna Graecia, and this period is generally seen as one of Etruscan decline – the beginning of the end of a long period of dominance. The motivation for the Gauls' movement south towards Rome, at least as presented in Livy, is ambiguous though. The general narrative which he presents of Gallic incursions ever further south into Italy is one based on a desire for land, and Livy seems to imply that this was also true for Brennus' Gauls. This would suggest that Brennus was travelling with a large group of Gauls, which likely included women, children, animals, etc., which was bent on conquest or at least settlement – an interpretation which was also presented by Polybius in his account of the event. However, there is also the ulterior motivation of service in the court of Dionysius I of Syracuse as mercenaries. This type of mercenary service was particularly common in the fourth century BC, as numerous recent studies have illustrated, and southern Italy in particular had a thriving mercenary economy. If this motivation represents the actual one (and the circumstantial evidence suggests that it was), then Brennus might not have been travelling with an entire tribe, including women and children, but rather a group of warriors who were setting out to make their fortune and then, perhaps, return home.

Whatever the actual makeup of the Gallic forces at Clusium, Allia and Rome, they were undoubtedly effective and evidently defeated the Roman forces in all three battles. At Clusium, this would not have taken much. Livy reported that three members of the Fabian clan had been sent to Clusium as ambassadors of Rome, but evidently joined the local forces and engaged in battle against the Gauls. The forces of Clusium, along with the Fabii, were quickly defeated, but this involvement by the Fabii supposedly provoked the Gauls into attacking Rome, leading to the city's eventual capture. While the reality of this portion of the narrative is entirely uncertain, and may either represent an anti-Fabian tradition (blaming them for the sack) or perhaps the activities of an independent clan-based army which merely happened to get involved, after defeating the forces of Clusium, the Gauls did evidently continue their march south, meeting the forces of Rome at the River Allia. The Roman army which faced off against them was led by six consular tribunes, including the three Fabii from Clusium in addition to Quintus Sulpicius Longus, Quintus Servilius and Publius Cornelius Maluginensis, and contained approximately 40,000 men. While it is likely that this estimate is exaggerated, the actual number of Romans present was clearly substantial, as the magnitude of the subsequent defeat was deeply etched into the Roman consciousness. During the battle, the Roman army was evidently spread thin in an attempt to match the frontage of the much larger Gallic force and was quickly routed, with the remnants of the army fleeing to both Rome and the recently captured city of Veii. After the defeat, the Gauls entered Rome virtually unopposed, except for the defences on the Capitoline. The sources then describe an epic siege of the Romans on the hill, with the rest of the city burning below. Included in the larger siege narrative is the famous anecdote of the geese, where the Gauls attempt to sneak up the side of the Capitoline hill but in doing so startle the geese who lived there, sacred to Juno, with the resultant noise alerting the Romans to the danger. In honour of this, the Romans later founded a temple to Juno Moneta (*moneta* from the Latin word *monere*, to warn) on the Capitoline, which ultimately became the mint at Rome. Eventually, however, the Senate was forced to negotiate a truce with the Gauls whereby they paid the Gallic leader Brennus 1,000lbs of gold.

What happened after the negotiations is slightly more problematic. One tradition states that the Romans simply paid the indemnity. This version often includes the anecdote that the Romans then discovered that the Gauls were using heavier weights than the standard typically used for weighing out the gold, but when the Romans complained Brennus supposedly threw his sword on top of the scales and uttered the phrase '*vae victis*' ('Woe to the conquered') in response. However, Livy offers a different version, followed by Plutarch, which claimed that while the Capitol was still besieged the Senate appointed as dictator the exiled Roman noble Camillus, who eventually arrived from Ardea with an army and, after summoning additional forces from Veii, went on to defeat the Gallic forces before the ransom could be paid. Diodorus provided another version in which the ransom was paid and the Gauls left the city, only to be defeated in a separate battle at Veascium later that year by Camillus, and the gold was then recovered. Polybius, meanwhile, offered yet another version where the bribe was paid and the Gauls simply returned home, an account which Livy actually supports in a later passage.

Camillus

An important, and yet incredibly enigmatic, figure in this entire narrative is Marcus Furius Camillus (traditionally lived *c*. 446–365 BC). Camillus, as he is commonly known, is probably one of the most important figures in early Roman history and yet also one of the most obscure. Described by Livy as a 'second founder' of Rome,[5] an attribution which is supported by Plutarch,[6] Camillus dominates the narrative *c*. 400 BC, and plays the leading role in both the siege and sack of Veii and Rome's recovery from the Gallic sack. His only notable absence is from the narrative of Rome's defeat itself, which is explained by his 'exile' just previous to that. He triumphed at least four times and held the dictatorship five times, along with the consular tribunate (multiple times) and the censorship – giving him a military and political career which was truly remarkable during this period. Indeed, rather like Tarquinius Superbus at the start of the fifth century BC, who seemed to feature amongst Rome's enemies in just about every battle, the figure of Camillus is ubiquitous in the narrative, appearing in a leading role in almost all of Rome's victories (although he is conspicuously absent from her losses).

Intriguingly, however, not all of the surviving sources for the early fourth century BC feature Camillus. Both Diodorus and Polybius, the latter of which is often seen as one of the more reliable historians, largely ignore Camillus and his achievements, which has led some scholars (when taken along with his arguably unbelievable résumé) to suggest that not only was the figure of Camillus exaggerated, he may have actually been largely invented. The mid-twentieth century scholar Georges Dumézil, for instance, argued that Camillus was not intended to be a historical figure at all but actually an *exemplum* created by later writers, which he associated with a hero of the goddess Aurora, who personified key Roman virtues during this period.[7] Others have taken a series of less extreme positions, but even the more optimistic scholars have generally been forced to admit that the record for Camillus most likely contains some significant elaboration. These points aside, it is clear that Camillus represents an important figure in, at least, the Roman memory of the period *c.* 400 BC. He seems to have embodied, somehow, the spirit or '*zeitgeist*' of the time and his actions, however much they were exaggerated by later storytellers and writers, were remembered as vital to Rome's development.

Historicity aside, Camillus does represent quite a *useful* figure in the narrative. As already noted, he was used in some versions of the story to assuage Roman honour during and after the sack, by defeating the Gauls and reclaiming Rome's gold. He also represented a powerful catalyst for Rome's recovery, as his victories in the 380s, 370s and 360s BC drove a prolonged period of Roman expansion and conquest. Camillus is an intriguing figure too in the internal political debates which raged in Rome during the 370s and 360s BC. Although a patrician and the most important figure in Roman politics at this time, Camillus is also presented as a facilitator of *concordia*, or peace, between the patricians and plebeians in the 'Struggle of the Orders', and specifically in the ten years of political unrest between 376 and 367 BC. Indeed, as a result of the *concordia ordinum* which Camillus achieved he is supposed to have founded and dedicated a temple to Concordia in the forum. In Livy's narrative, which is our main source for this period (Dionysius's history being unfortunately fragmentary for these years), Camillus seems to represent both sides in the debate at various times although, as Momigliano and others have noted, his involvement is likely to represent, at least in part, a late Republican attempt to rationalize the events. But it is exactly this ability to represent both sides of a matter which makes him so appealing. Camillus is at once an Archaic warleader who is evidently mobile (as seen by his exile and subsequent return to power in Rome) and backed by a powerful *gens* (the *Furii*). His power base and position therefore harken back to the fifth century BC and the powerful, warlike raiding *gentes* which dominated the period. However, in Rome he also occupies a prime position in the new, state-based system – acting as both a consular tribune and censor, but never as a *praetor*. The closest he comes to that position is as the dictator, a position which he holds multiple times, and which might have served as the template for the later consulship. Camillus is therefore a liminal or transitional figure in the narrative, which both represents the old, archaic model of power and new, state-based way of operating, which includes both the patricians and the plebeians.

Camillus' role in Roman history *c.* 400 BC is therefore an important one. Whether or not he represents a real figure (the evidence from the *fasti* suggests that he was) and whether or not all of his achievements are real (here the evidence is far from convincing), Camillus does seem to illustrate an interesting phenomenon – the final integration of Latium's gentilicial elite into Rome's social, political and military systems after the Gallic sack. A previously mobile war leader, who may have been exiled (or simply left for greener pastures), Camillus was invited to return to Rome in the years following the sack of Rome and played a key role in the city's return to greatness. This hints that the urban community of Rome recognized that having a figure like Camillus, along with his evidently powerful group of followers, was important given the defeat by the Gauls. And it also suggests that figures such as Camillus, despite the 'old-fashioned' or archaic nature of his power base, found ways to make Rome's new military and political system work for him as well. For Camillus, this was largely done through the mechanism of the dictatorship, but his role in establishing the *concordia ordinum* may also suggest that this type of figure was increasingly finding areas to compromise and establish a system which worked for both sides of the 'Struggle of the Orders'. So although the figure of Camillus is problematic in strictly historical terms, he may illustrate some important developments in Rome during this period – and the strongest evidence for this is how well his actions and behaviour align with the rest of Rome's reactions to the Gallic sack.

Rome's Internal Reaction

Rome's invitation to Camillus to return to Rome, supposedly issued while the Capitoline hill was still under siege by the Gauls, is generally representative of Rome's attitude during the years immediately following the defeat. While the city and her increasingly stable collection of clans/ *gentes* had previously let local politics dominate and individual ambitions dictate both domestic and foreign policy, in the years after the sack Rome emerged with a new direction and drive. And, as with the recalling of Camillus from Ardea, this direction was based on immediately securing and expanding her military capabilities, probably in order to prevent a future defeat by the Gauls. All previous squabbles were largely forgotten – this new threat required a concerted effort from everyone.

Rome's sudden, and entirely reasonable, interest in expanding her military capabilities took a number of different forms. As already noted, the recall of Camillus from his 'exile' in Ardea seems to have been the first of these, but even this was part of a much larger attempt to bring the clans who lived around the city together into a more stable union. As suggested in the previous chapter, the powerful clans of Latium, and Central Italy more generally, had already begun the long process of slowly settling down and permanently associating themselves with various communities back in the sixth and fifth centuries BC. This can be linked to changes in the economy and an increased focus on land and agriculture, in addition to the rise of the urban centres themselves. However, as the exile of Camillus indicates (and whether this represented a true exile or merely the movement of a powerful clan leader is still debatable), prominent figures were still able to move around the region and retain most, if not all, of their power and influence, suggesting that this process was ongoing. During the first half of the fourth century BC, however, Rome saw the rise of a distinctive 'Roman Nobility' – or group of clans who would go on to dominate Roman politics for the rest of the Republican period, to the exclusion of others. Associated with the closing of the patriciate in the second half of the fifth century BC, which marked the establishment of a distinct 'patrician' group in Rome, the creation of the 'Roman Nobility', although still partly based on kinship, was predicated on a new set of social norms where glory and social power were attained largely through holding positions within Rome's civic structure. Although obviously in its infancy during this period, as scholars like Matthias Gelzer identified back in the early twentieth century, the fourth century BC witnessed the origins of a group, who were described as *clarissimi* or *principes civitatis* by later sources, whose position was due almost entirely to their family history of holding the key magistracies in Rome.[8] Unfortunately, the nuances of the earliest incarnation of this group are likely lost to us forever, given the nature of the sources for this period, but this development seems to be the result of the city developing a particular, mutually beneficial relationship with certain families, whereby the longstanding competition which had existed between them for glory was moved from outside the city – in the form of raiding, mortuary practices, etc. – to inside the city, and a competition over magistracies.

This relationship clearly benefited the community, as it firmly linked the local clans and their military strength to the city for the long term, but

it is initially unclear what the advantage might be for the clans. Although
the clans which had settled around Rome would increasingly have had
their interests aligned with those of the community anyway, with the
result that maximising the military capabilities of the community would
have also benefited them, the continuing existence of mobile clans in
Latium, who would have been able to simply pick up and leave if the
Gauls returned (as perhaps Camillus did in 390 BC), suggests that this was
not enough for everyone. The result of this situation is yet another period
of political tension within Rome, and another flare up of the 'Struggle
of the Orders', as the powerful, rural clans and the urban community
once again attempted to find some middle ground. The default during
the first half of the fourth century BC seems to have been the use of the
consular tribunate, with all that that entailed, although the office of the
dictatorship was also increasingly utilized, seemingly as a short-term
solution to this issue. The dictatorship allowed the return of many of
the Archaic prerogatives of the praetorship, including *imperium* (and
the associated right to triumph) and so would have been appealing to
the region's gentilicial elite, but could be used alongside the consular
tribunate and therefore maximised Rome's military might. However, it is
clear that this was a short-term solution and one which was not wholly
satisfactory to either side. As a result, in 367 BC, the Romans created a
new magistracy as a long-term fix: the revamped consulship.

Rome's late Republican historians clearly viewed the introduction of
the consulship in 367 BC as the reintroduction or reinstatement of the
old praetorship, and indeed they often (confusingly for modern scholars)
called the Archaic praetorship 'the consulship'. There are some very
good reasons for this, the most obvious being the return of the regular
grant of *imperium*. The powers of the praetorship and the consulship
were both somehow governed by a grant of *imperium*, which still involved
the curiate assembly, meaning that their relationship to the community
was roughly similar and that both could be seen as descendants of the *rex*.
Additionally, both magistracies carried the auspices, or religious powers,

and were collegial in nature, with two consuls being elected each year after 367 BC, which roughly mirrors the previous arrangement with the *praetors* – although it is entirely possible that there were more than two *praetors* in many years of the fifth century BC, though the tradition of *consules suffecti* (so-called 'replacement consuls/*praetors*' who are sometimes recorded) and the 'cleaned up' Augustan-era *fasti* make this impossible to determine with any certainty. The offices were also dominated by the same group of families, at least initially.

There were, however, some key differences between the offices as well. First, and most importantly for the literary sources, the new consulship was open to the plebeians. From Livy's narrative, this development represents nothing more than a (admittedly very important) political compromise but, based on our discussion of Rome's army so far, the importance of this in more practical terms should also be evident. Allowing the plebeians, even plebeian elites, to hold the consulship indicates that the basis of power for this office was no longer a clan or *gens* but rather the community. As a result, this office could arguably be considered a closer descendant of the consular tribunate which immediately preceded it, than the Archaic praetorship or the *rex*. Without well-established clans or *gentes* to act as the core of their military forces (and it does seem that the plebeians did not have proper *gentes*, although they would have obviously have had some sort of family and client-based structure), the new plebeian consuls were entirely dependent on recruitment through the community in order to form their armies. This, however, creates problems when one considers the re-emergence of *imperium*. As discussed, Archaic *imperium* was most likely a sort of contract between the community and an external war leader and his clan, which bound together the two entities in a mutually beneficial relationship. The question then arises of why would *imperium* be needed for the consulship, if the office was a community-based one? The answer to this question is 'compromise'.

It seems clear that the consular tribunes were reasonably effective militarily, as this was the office that the Romans reverted to for regular military commands after the Gallic sack when they needed success the most. From the point of view of Rome's powerful clans and *gentes*, however, this system did not suit their social needs. The praetorship, and its *imperium*, had formed an increasingly important part of their internal competition for social and political prestige. While achieving the consular tribunate was evidently also something which was thought to be valuable, as they did compete for this as well, it seemed to lack the appeal of the praetorship, with the right to triumph and the range of powers and privileges associated with the grants of *imperium* and *auspicium*. In the new, post-390 BC environment, this level of power was only attainable through the office of the dictator, which was irregularly appointed and dominated by a few individuals (like Camillus). So it seems likely that the city's gentilicial elite were eager for a return to the praetorship in some form. On the other hand, the community and its plebeian elite had been gaining in power during this period and had demonstrated their ability as generals in the consular tribunate, and seem to have gotten a taste for the rewards of military success themselves. Given this position, they were unlikely to want to see a return to magistracy which would once again have them locked out. So the end result was the creation of the consulship (*consul*, likely derived from *con* and *sul*, meaning 'those who go together'), which represented a compromise that effectively combined the best parts of the two offices – the military capabilities and community basis of the consular tribunate, and the power and prestige of the preatorship – into a single office open to both groups. It is clear that this compromise was not reached easily, despite its eminent practicality, as attested by the supposed ten years of unrest before its advent and the various debates after (particularly concerning the auspices). This new arrangement would have also resulted in some dramatic changes to the grant of *imperium* and indeed, even apart from the changes outlined above, scholars have been increasingly pushing for 367 BC as marking a key moment of change and evolution for *imperium* and the *lex curiata de imperio*. After 367 BC, *imperium* and the *lex curiata de imperio* (the law passed by the curiate assembly which governed it) were no longer needed to bind an external war leader to the community, and as a result they both seem to have taken on a more ritual or religious connotation, which is what was carried on into the late Republic.

For the past 100 years and more, scholars have tried to unravel the nature of Republican *imperium* and the *lex curiata de imperio*, particularly as it existed in the mid- to late Republic, and have increasingly come to the conclusion that both the grant and the law which governed it should be considered to be largely ritual in nature. Although passing the *lex* and having *imperium* officially granted by the *curiae* was generally seen as the 'right thing to do', its absence did not seem to affect the power of the magistrate in any real terms. This was most famously recorded by Cicero in his account of Appius Claudius, where he stated that:

> Appius used some time back to repeat in conversation, and afterwards said openly, even in the senate, that if he were allowed to carry a law in the *comitia curiata*, he would draw lots with his colleague for their provinces; but if no *curiatian* law were passed, he would make an arrangement with his colleague and succeed you: that a *curiatian* law was a proper thing for a consul, but was not a necessity: that since he was in possession of a province by a decree of the senate, he should have *imperium* in virtue of the Cornelian law until such time as he entered the city.[9]

Of far more significance during the middle and late Republic were the religious ramifications of the *lex curiata de imperio*, which may have increasingly related to the auspices and the ability to perform certain rituals. Although this did not affect the ability to command an army during this period, it did seem to influence the perceived relationship with the gods. This was still an important aspect as it was raised in debates in 445 BC and again in 362 BC, when the ill-fated plebeian consul L. Gernucius, who was the first plebeian consul to go to war under his own auspices, was defeated and killed by the Hernici. However, the nature of *imperium* and military command had clearly changed in Rome by the middle of the fourth century BC, and things were increasingly focusing inward on the community.

Connected with this inward focus and the shift in military command, there may also have been a gradual shift in military equipment and formation. This will be discussed in detail in the next chapter, but several points connected with both Rome's command structure and the influence of the Gauls are worth highlighting now. Looking first at command structure, the reinterpretation of *imperium* and Rome's increasing reliance on community-based forces after 367 BC did not mean that its military forces (or the Central Italian clans and *gentes*) started to fight in a completely different manner or tactical formation – although it did probably result in a slightly more unified arrangement. As already argued, it is highly unlikely that Rome ever utilized a hoplite phalanx, and in fact Rome's armed forces, such as they were, likely utilized the more flexible, and probably amorphous, tactical formations favoured by the *gentes* for raiding. Although there are no specific descriptions of these formations in the sources, looking at other ancient examples (most notably from Spain in the third and second centuries BC) it has been argued that they most likely resembled 'dense clouds' which expanded and contracted during the course of a battle.[10] As Rome's army increasingly unified and expanded during the course of the fourth century BC, the community would have had to find a way to effectively utilize soldiers and units used to fighting in this manner. Consequently, it is likely that the mid-fourth century BC represents the likely point of origin for a 'proto-manipular legion'. Although it is unlikely to have featured all the nuances and organizational details of its later counterpart, the Roman army of the mid-fourth century would have probably contained a number of 'handfuls' (*manipuli*) or groups of men, which were the descendants of the archaic war bands of the fifth century BC, increasingly fighting in a co-ordinated fashion.

The fourth century BC also saw the introduction of some new military equipment in the Roman army, which seems to have come from two different sources. The first source was local, and was perhaps a result of an increasing number of urban, and probably 'middle class', men engaging in warfare under the banners of the consular tribunes, and later consuls. These men, although by no means poor (arguably analogous with the *zeugitae* or 'hoplite-class' in Greece), were not from the wealthiest segments of society either and also had very little previous connection to warfare. As a result, we can probably link to these soldiers the increasing use of simple but functional helmets, like the increasingly popular *montefortino* type, and a general 'democratization' of military equipment across the board. Associated with this is the use of a new type of heavy javelin, which makes it appearance in Central Italy at this time. Prior to this time, javelins are rather hard to identify in the archaeological record. Although spears had most likely been thrown for centuries, if not millennia, in Italy, for the most part they were of the 'multi-purpose' variety – spears which could be used as either a thrusting weapon or a thrown one. During the course of the fourth century BC, however, there is increasing evidence for purpose-designed heavy javelins being used throughout Italy – a development which may be associated with the growing number of Gauls in the peninsula. Although by no means unique to the Gauls, the type of heavy javelin which appears in the fourth century BC in Italy is very close to the type of weapon favoured by those living in the modern-day regions of southern Austria and southern France, just the other side of the Alps. It is therefore probable that this military development arrived with the Gallic tribesmen in Italy and was slowly adopted by the Italic peoples.

Finally, this period also witnessed the construction of Rome's first, substantial city walls which completely surrounded the settlement. Known as Rome's 'Servian Walls', after a misattribution to Rome's sixth *rex* who was also credited with building walls around the city, the Servian Walls were probably begun in 378 BC – as Livy states that in this year 'further debts were incurred through the levying of a tax to build a wall of hewn stone, which the censors had contracted for.'[11] Built from *Grotta Oscura tufo* taken from quarries near the city of Veii and constructed using ashlar blocks, the fortifications extended a full 11km. Many of the blocks bore Greek masons' marks, indicating that the Romans may have brought in specialists from Magna Graecia to help build them – something which is arguably unsurprising given the Hellenistic style of the walls. Indeed, the walls were truly massive in scale. A full 4 metres thick, and even today reaching a height of over 10 metres in places, the walls enclosed an area of approximately 426 hectares, meaning that they were on a par with the largest settlement fortifications in the western Mediterranean. The walls were so massive that they may have taken at least twenty-five years to construct, as Livy's entry from the year 353 BC implies. These were Rome's main fortifications throughout the Republican period, and were the walls which Hannibal famously viewed and considered attacking during the Second Punic War.

The likely reasons behind the construction of the walls are many and varied, but the threat of another Gallic attack was undoubtedly top amongst them. While Rome's previous collection of *aggeres* and *fossae* (ramparts and ditches) had evidently been at least reasonably effective against the small-scale raids of Latin clans and Italic tribes, the threat posed by the Gauls obviously necessitated a change in approach. Rome could no longer rely on a piecemeal set of fortifications which left significant gaps in her defences. Additionally, as scholars have recognized for years, city walls often represent far more than a military obstacle. City walls, and particularly full circuit walls on the scale of Rome's new fortifications, are often thought to draw a line between 'us' and 'them' in the terrain, and as such are key markers of civic identity and civic cohesion. The construction of such walls around Rome in the early fourth century BC thus makes sense culturally and socially, and was in keeping with Rome's larger programme of self-definition.

Rome's External Reaction

Rome's increased unity and internal cohesion in the aftermath of the Gallic sack can also be seen in her changing relationship with the rest of the Latins and the other peoples in Central Italy. While Rome had previously fought a series of low-level wars with various communities and tribes in Central Italy, these had generally had minimal long-term consequences or repercussions. Settlements would be raided and wealth taken but, for the most part, there was no attempt to exert control over the defeated peoples in the long term or incorporate them into the Roman state. During the fourth century BC, however, Rome became increasingly expansionist and interested in the capture and control of land and communities. This seems to have been the result of two concurrent developments in Roman society, visible in Rome's actions with Veii at the turn of the century, which included an increased interest in land as being both valuable and a viable spoil of war, and also a strategic interest in increasing her manpower reserves.

Rome's desire for land seems to have dramatically increased during the course of the fourth and early third centuries BC, with Roman territory (*ager Romanus*, and specifically *ager publicus*) expanding massively during this period, largely through military conquest. This growth was exponential, with Rome directly controlling a territory of a few hundred square kilometres *c.* 390 BC, approximately 8,500 km² by 340 BC and over 26,000 km² by 264 BC.[12] This is not to say that Rome's interests did not extend further afield than a few hundred square kilometres prior to 390 BC, as the 'carrying capacity' of this land (the amount of food which it was able to produce) would have likely been unable to support a city the size of Rome in this period, and Rome's armies clearly ranged further afield. However, the land outside of the *ager Romanus antiquus* (the area within 5 miles of the *pomerium*, or ritual boundary of Rome), possibly even including parts of the tribal zones and the earliest sections of *ager publicus*, should probably be considered 'liminal' at best. Although Romans – and Roman armies – may have moved across it, so did other groups in Latium. Used largely for grazing herds and flocks, or heavily forested (as the vast majority of Central Italy was at this time), much of this land was effectively unclaimed during the Archaic period, as it was not economically viable, or indeed feasible, to do so. It was only with the advent of more intensive agricultural practices during this period, coupled with the creation of a more cohesive Roman state, that it was in Rome's best interests to permanently claim land as 'Roman'. Consequently, this period witnessed the true birth of the Roman Empire, as a territorial entity, and the beginnings of Roman land-use policies (and problems) which would shape many of the events of the late Republic.

Economics were clearly driving some of this expansion. The larger developments within Roman agricultural practices which had featured back in the fifth century BC (the gradual settling down of the clans, the increase in investment in agriculture and irrigation, etc.) all seem to have continued unabated into the fourth century BC. This, coupled with an increase in population, resulted in an ever-increasing demand for land during this period as individual Romans struggled to climb the economic ladder, clans endeavoured to control this emerging form of wealth and the community as a whole found itself needing to feed more and more mouths. With the available nearby land already occupied, and without a strong tradition of seafaring to allow maritime colonization on a scale similar to that of the Greeks, the Romans turned to conquest to deal with the issue – although this was not as straightforward as it might seem. While Rome's conquests of the early fourth century BC did start to satiate the land hunger of the population, it was tempered by a few factors – most notably Rome's desire to maintain her military strength. As a result, during the fourth century BC Rome did not utilize 'colonization' particularly heavily, which is often considered surprising as this was how the Romans are usually thought to have controlled captured land. But while Rome supposedly established four new colonies in Latium during the 380s BC, between 380 and 338 BC there were no records of any Roman colony foundations. Indeed, scholars like E.T. Salmon, in his epic volume on Roman colonization, was forced into a series of convoluted arguments to explain this decline, with 'diminished military need', an 'estrangement' between Rome and the Latins and possible 'problems of administration and assimilation' all possibly playing a role.[13] Although Salmon may have been correct with some of his caveats, the main reason for this decline was likely that early Roman colonies, like their Greek counterparts, seem to have become independent communities after they were founded. As a result, while they might have harboured some sentimental attachments to their mother community, they could not necessarily be trusted to automatically act in Rome's best interests, let alone as allies. This type of behaviour by 'colonies' of Rome can be seen time and again during the sixth, fifth and early fourth centuries BC, with colonies regularly rebelling and almost never coming to Rome's aid in times of trouble. So while colonization might be an easy way to distribute land to Romans, it was not in Rome's best interests to do so in a time when she was evidently trying to secure her position and expand her military manpower. As a result, Rome seems to have spent much of the early fourth century BC trying to find an answer to this conundrum – how could she expand territorially, while still maintaining (and indeed growing) her citizen base?

Rome attempted a few different mechanisms to get around this issue, all of which were maintained in some form or another into the late Republican period. The first was simply to expand her tribal structure. This was what Rome did after the Gallic sack with the territory and people of Veii. Although she had only recently captured the community, Rome incorporated the *ager Veientanus* and its population by dividing it up and creating four new rural tribes which then formed part of Rome's citizen body. This would have immediately increased Rome's manpower reserves, although it did have some obvious drawbacks – most notably giving the recently-captured Veientines a say in Roman politics – and it was really only a feasible model of inclusion for communities and land in the immediate vicinity of Rome. In the 380s BC, Rome attempted to found colonies, but quickly stopped this practice because, while they helped to alleviate the pressure on land, they also drained Rome's military manpower as it is clear that these colonies (Satricum, Sutrium, Nepete and Setia) were of the archaic type and quickly exerted their independence. This led to one of Rome's key innovations, the foundation of the first *municipium* at Tusculum in 380 BC. Following its capture, the community of Tusculum was incorporated into the Roman state through a grant of *civitas sine suffragio* (citizenship without voting rights) and the community was dubbed a *municipium*. The people of Tusculum therefore had something resembling dual citizenship, as they were also considered citizens or residents of Tusculum, and the community was allowed to self-govern as it had before. However, whenever a need arose, the people of Tusculum were also subject to conscription and service in the Roman army. This innovation seems to have addressed some of Rome's manpower issues and the question of how to increase her military base without giving up control. It did not, however, help with the land issue – although it did provide a possible model. Indeed, Rome's approach to captured land from the mid-fourth century BC onwards seems to have followed the basic premise behind the creation of *municipia* – allowing a certain degree of local flexibility while maintaining central control. This was primarily done through the increased use of *ager publicus* (public land). The *ager publicus* was usually captured land which remained under the ownership and control of the state, but which could be utilized by any Roman who wished (and non-Romans for a fee). This land was very quickly dominated by the elite clans, as laws as early as the 360s BC indicate, but was supposedly open to all Romans and would have offered the (on paper at least) perfect solution to Rome's land problem.

The creation of *municipia* and the use of *ager publicus* on a wide scale were only possible in the post-390 BC political environment of Rome, where a strengthened community ethos dominated and an increasingly community-centred army fought for land which could be utilized by all. Together, these measures helped to shape the way in which Rome increasingly dealt with the various communities and peoples in Central Italy, and further abroad, by ensuring that her own needs were met (in the fourth century BC this entailed both land and manpower) through maintaining a certain level of central control but allowing a high degree of local flexibility. Rome's needs would naturally change over time, which resulted in new methods of control and exploitation. For instance, by the late fourth century BC, Roman citizenship and Roman identity seem to have reached a point where true citizen colonies were possible, which were utilized by Rome where more control was needed than that offered by *municipia* (this will be discussed in the subsequent chapters). In the third century BC, when Rome's conquests were increasingly distant and far-flung, the state developed a new model of control – the creation of *provincia* (provinces) – which met Rome's needs of strategic security and wealth. But all of these developments were still guided by the same principles which underpinned the first steps which Rome took towards empire in the early fourth century BC.

Conclusion

The Gallic sack of Rome can be best described as a catalyst for Rome. Although the arrival of the Gauls can possibly be credited with a few developments in its own right, most notably the use of the heavy javelin, its biggest impact was in accelerating a number of existing trends in Roman society. This included bringing the community, and particularly the local clans, together into a single, cohesive whole and unifying them all under the banner of Rome. Although this process was well under way previously, the Gallic sack seems to have demonstrated in no uncertain terms that the archaic way of life, and particularly the clan-based approach to war, was no longer a viable option. In the aftermath of the sack, Rome did everything she could to increase her manpower and develop a military model to protect against further attacks. This included incorporating new peoples into her citizen body (and military ranks) via the creation of new tribes and *municpia*, along with the full-time reversion to the consular tribunate and eventually the creation of the consulship.

Rome's increased internal unity and cohesion also allowed a more concerted approach to land acquisition and ownership, generally exploited through the creation of *ager publicus*, which gradually developed into a territorial empire. Evidently initiated to satiate the Romans' increased appetite for land, but tempered by the desire to maintain her manpower reserves and control both the territory and those occupying it (in contrast to previous practice), Rome very quickly carved out a massive Central Italian empire during the course of the fourth century BC. This led the city into increased conflicts with a number of Italian peoples, including the other Latin communities and tribes, as her aggressive and expansionist policies started to impact upon them. This ultimately resulted in a series of wars against the Latins, Samnites, Etruscans and Greeks of Magna Graecia in the second half of the fourth century BC, which further shaped Rome's military and imperial designs.

Chapter 5

Rome and the Latins

R ome's relationship with the rest of the Latins was very like that which often exists between siblings – and indeed this is an appropriate analogy, given that all the Latins (including Rome) seem to have shared a common origin and developed out of the same ancestral culture in Italy (the Proto-Villanovans). Sometimes friendly, often tumultuous, full of rivalry and bickering, and yet also capable of unified and concerted action – particularly when faced with an outside threat – Rome and the Latins present modern scholars with a complex web of connections, associations and influences which is incredibly hard to disentangle. This relationship was not based on a treaty (although Rome and the Latins did sign more than one) or on strict legal or even ritual rules and laws (although these too did exist), but instead it developed over many centuries and is, like any other family dynamic, almost impossible for us as outsiders to fully understand.

Rome was, of course, a city in Latium and as such was part of a larger Latin culture, which was distinguished not only by its language – Latin – but also by a rough geographic affiliation ('Latin' is derived from the word '*latus*', which means 'flat' or 'broad' and seems to have referred to the coastal plain which makes up the majority of the region), along with certain broad cultural characteristics, including burial practices and religion. As a result, the archaeology of early Rome is largely indistinguishable from that of other communities in Latium. Its people lived in the same types of huts (and later houses) as the other Latins, grew the same types of crops, made the same types of art and buried their dead in the same ways. Added to this are a range of connections evident in the literary evidence, including a long tradition of Latin unity, with the Latins all supposedly coming together once a year for a festival of Jupiter Latiaris, the *Feriae Latinae*, to discuss matters of mutual concern, make alliances, settle grievances, arrange marriages and even agree on joint military actions. There are also the archaic Latin rights of intermarriage (*ius conuibium*) and the ability to travel between and settle in the different communities (*ius exilia*). When this is combined with the tradition for mobile clans, which seem to have moved from community to community in addition to facilitating the trade which ran through the region, one increasingly gets the impression of Latium (including Rome) as being far more homogenous than often thought. While there were clearly groups and communities with distinct identities in Latium, they were all part of a much broader social and cultural matrix, which was kept fluid and active by the region's mobile clans. In this context, Rome was just one of many Latin communities, with little to distinguish it on the surface – although the city did have a few unique characteristics which would serve it well in the long run.

Rome's position on the Tiber River meant that it controlled much of the trade running through the region, as it sat astride the main fording point on the river and therefore guarded the gateway into Etruria. Rome also had access to a number of natural resources, including clay and (famously) salt, in addition to nearby farmland which allowed it to develop into a major industrial and commercial centre. But overall, the similarity of the archaeological record for early Rome to that found at other Latin communities clearly suggests that the story of 'Roman exceptionalism' which pervades the literary evidence – that the Romans, as the mythical descendants of Aeneas and the Trojans, were always unique and destined for greatness – was a myth created in hindsight. Even as late as the sixth or early fifth centuries BC, it is uncertain whether the Latins (or indeed the Romans themselves) would have predicted Rome's rise to power. The city was obviously doing quite well for itself, but so were many other Latin communities, and a certain equilibrium seems to have been reached in the region.

But Rome *did* rise to power and prominence during the course of the fifth and early fourth centuries, and indeed by the middle of the fourth century BC her emerging empire came into direct conflict with the rest of the Latin peoples over their increasingly divergent goals and interests. This conflict led to the Latin War, or 'Latin Uprising', from which Rome ultimately emerged victorious in 338 BC. This victory, and the series of alliances which developed out of it, went on to set the stage for Rome's victories over the Samnites, against Pyrrhus and ultimately the Carthaginians in the third century BC. Although often ignored in favour of Rome's flashier achievements in the middle and late Republic, Rome's evolving relationship with the Latins in the fifth and fourth centuries BC shaped her approach to citizenship, warfare and military tactics, and ultimately to empire.

The Traditional Model

The traditional interpretation of Rome's relationship with the Latins is, like many aspects of early Roman history, largely a product of late Republican bias and historical hindsight. It presents Rome and the rest of Latium as two sides in an unequal partnership. On the one side was Rome, generally considered the most important and powerful community in the region which (it was thought at least) was able to exert a certain degree of control over much of the region from the early Regal period onward. On the other side were the Latins, a motley collection of tribes and communities which, even put together, seem to have never been able to match the strength of Rome. They shared a common birth with Rome, along with a common language and culture, which afforded them a certain level of respect – or perhaps tolerance – in the eyes of Rome's later historians. But the Latins were generally thought of as small children who were trying to play with the big kids – never real threats, even in 340 BC when they went into full revolt, but a group which must be treated carefully and differently because of the longstanding cultural connections which existed with Rome. They were family.

This interpretation makes some sense when you consider the position and perspective of historians such as Livy, and even his predecessors like Fabius Pictor writing in the late third and early second century BC. For these men the Latins had always been close allies and effectively subsidiary communities to Rome. Even the earliest Roman historian, Fabius Pictor, would have been writing generations after Rome's Italian empire had been established and while its Mediterranean empire was on the rise. From this vantage point, they would have seen the Latins as but a shadow of their former selves. Roman and Latin communities were dotted across the region of Latium, intermixed, and the line between Roman and Latin citizenships, while still visible, was the most blurred of any in Rome's burgeoning empire. Many Latin communities had a type of modified Roman citizenship, citizenship without voting rights (*civitas sine suffragio*), in addition to their local affiliation, and they still carried the Archaic Latin rights of intermarriage and exile which the Romans ascribed to as well. By the mid to late Republic, the economies of the Latin communities were entirely dependent on the needs and whims of Rome's massive population; their farms existed as small pockets of land in an ever-growing sea of *ager Romanus* and *ager publicus* (and indeed they sometimes utilized this land, for a fee, themselves), and many Romans also lived in or around Latin communities and vice versa. In this time period, the Romans and the Latins did indeed exist in a bilateral relationship whereby being 'a Latin' effectively meant being a slightly inferior Roman – clearly better than everyone else and with a special relationship to Rome, but not quite up to the level of real Romans.

This understanding of Rome's relationship with the rest of Latium has coloured our literary sources' interpretation of the earlier periods of Roman history, with the result that Rome was always seen to have an unequal relationship with the rest of Latium, usually embodied by the Latin League or the federation of Latin states. Control of Latium's military forces, such as they were (and we will address this issue in due course), supposedly alternated between Rome and the rest of the Latins – meaning that Rome controlled the unified forces every other year. Rome is also recorded as speaking for the Latins in early treaties, most notably with Carthage, and generally dictating terms to the rest of the region. It is only in a few very specific instances, typically interpreted as rebellions, that the Latins seem to rise up and exert their rights – usually only to be crushed by the might of Rome. This quite famously happened at the Battle of Lake Regillus in the early fifth century BC, again in the early fourth century BC and in 340–338 BC ending in Rome's final victory over the various communities and tribes of the region. Despite the unanimity of the literary sources on this position, scholars have still often wondered how realistic this interpretation of Rome's relationship with the Latins really is. Rome was a big community and indeed was likely the biggest in Latium, in terms of both population and land area, from the sixth century BC onward. But was Rome really powerful enough to take on the rest of the Latins and win? And if so, why does Rome have just as much trouble fighting against individual Latin communities (Fidenae, Praeneste, etc.) as she does against the entirety of the Latins or the Latin League? These questions can only be answered by delving into the very complex issues of 'who were the Latins' and 'what was the Latin League'.

When Roman sources use the term 'the Latins' (*Latini* or *nomen Latinum*, 'Latin name'), most modern scholars take it for granted that they are referring to the inhabitants of Latium as represented by the Latin League – a loose federation of communities and clans which parallels the Etruscan League to the north. The literary origins of this group go way back into the hazy period before Rome itself was even founded, as all of the communities in *Latium Vetus* ('Old Latium'), including Rome, were thought to be colonies of Alba Longa, one of the communities in the Alban hills located in the centre of the region. Although they are unlikely to represent actual colonies, this mythical memory may actually preserve a kernel of truth as the late Bronze and early Iron Age did see a gradual shift in settlement patterns from locations in the Alban hills, which were defensible but also isolated, down to the coastal plains in the west and river valleys in the east, likely driven by both trade and agriculture – although it is also possible that the connection to Alba Longa was used simply to justify the regular meeting site of the Latin League in these hills. Always thirty in number, although who was included in this figure seems to vary depending on both the source and time period, these communities were then thought to have shared a common origin, which explained their similar culture and language, and maintained a relationship even after the mother community of Alba Longa was supposedly destroyed by Rome's third *rex*, Tullus Hostilius. The nature of this relationship seems to have been mysterious even to the Romans (no surprise, given that they were looking back over almost 500 years without any solid evidence!), and only a few pieces of information are given about it. There seems to have been a regular – most likely annual – meeting of the *nomen Latinum*, possibly at the site of Aricia, although it was later moved to Ferentina. The sources clearly envisaged Rome dominating both the meeting and the Latins in general, although the few anecdotes which are given suggest a more chaotic and perhaps equal environment. The most famous incident involving the Latin League and the meeting at Ferentina occurred in the reign of Tarquinius Superbus, Rome's final *rex*, when he supposedly arranged to have the Latin noble Turnus Herdonius framed. Tarquin is also credited by Livy (1.52) with reorganizing the league into a more regular military alliance, although the evidence for this is problematic at best – particularly given the later behaviour of the League.

The evidence for the Latin League, or at least a formal relationship between the Latins, gets much better once we enter the Republican period. In the early years of the fifth century BC (traditionally 493 BC), the Latins, along with the Romans, supposedly signed the *Foedus Cassianum* (the Treaty of Cassius, named after Spurius Cassius) which dictated the basics of the relationship between the Latins for the next century and a half. Put up on a bronze tablet in the forum, which was still visible in the time of Cicero (Cic. *Balb.* 53), the treaty is summarized by Dionysius (Dion. Hal. *Ant. Rom.* 6.95) as promising peace between the Romans and the Latins, creating a defensive alliance between the groups, guaranteeing equal distribution of spoils in any joint military ventures and settling some economic disputes. The bilateral way in which Dionysius describes these terms has been taken by many as indicating that Rome was not part of the Latin League at this time, perhaps a result of the city falling under the influence of the Etruscans to the north (both the Tarquins and Lars Porsenna of Clusium's involvement in Rome have been advanced as evidence of this) and indeed this might explain why the Romans had fought against the Latins at the Battle of Lake Regillus only a few years previously. However, this may simply represent an unintended consequence of Dionysius' literary style; as his history was focused on Rome, he generally presented treaties involving Rome as bilateral for the sake of emphasis and comprehension, and elsewhere he seems to indicate a more diverse arrangement with a multitude of entities (Dion. Hal. *Ant. Rom.* 6.63–65). Moving forward into the fifth century BC, it becomes entirely uncertain how the treaty was interpreted at the time, as Rome and various Latin communities seem to be regularly in conflict during this period and there is little direct evidence of a defensive alliance (or at least a particularly effective one) being in place. Apart from the few direct references (Liv. 3.22; Dion. Hal. *Ant. Rom.* 9.13, etc.), the Latins are merely assumed to have been active alongside the Romans, although there is little evidence to suggest that this actually occurred.

Although the Latins (including the Romans) rarely seemed to have helped each other out in times of military need, and in fact were just as often at each other's throats, there did seem to be a system in place to allow unified military action focused on the institution of the Latin dictator. Derived from the verb *dictare* ('to command'), the existence of a Latin dictator is well attested in the sources and seems to have resembled the Roman version of the office in that he was supposedly given supreme command of the Latin League's forces for a period of six months. But apart from being chosen at the annual meeting of the league at the Lucus Ferentina (the antiquarian Cincius recorded that this happened as late as the year 340 BC, *Fest.* 276L), very little else is known about either the nature of the dictatorship or the Latin army. Although various models have been put forward, the general consensus is that the Latin army would have probably retained the federal organization of the league itself, with each community, clan or tribe existing as a separate unit – and indeed it is likely that all three types of entities would have been present. The Latin League clearly included communities like Rome, but the thirty *prisci Latini* (old Latins) of the league also seem to have included clans or *gentes* and, after the 480s BC, the tribal people of the Hernici as well. Each of these groups would have, presumably, been organized and fought independently, albeit under the overarching *imperium* (or similar power) of the dictator.

Despite the irregular use of the Latin dictatorship, and the evidently flexible interpretation of the 'defensive alliance' and 'perpetual peace' mentioned by Dionysius in his account of the *foedus Cassianum*, there are also some practical reasons for this type of system existing in the fifth century BC. Although each Latin entity, be it a community, tribe or clan, obviously had its own unique set of interests, the entire region of Latium was increasingly under threat during the fifth century BC by peoples from the mountainous interior of the peninsula. These invading tribes, like the Aequi and the Volsci in Latium along with the Samnites further south, put increasing pressure on the region's communities and clans as they came west looking for both booty and land to settle on. While the *prisci Latini* continued to squabble and raid amongst themselves, as siblings often do, they also seem to have recognized the regional threat that these external entities represented and the few times when a unified Latin army is explicitly attested in the sources for the fifth century BC, it is generally facing off against these types of foes. But occasional unified actions evidently did not stop the regular cycle of raiding which existed between the Latin clans and communities, as the literary record indicates. Rome, her clans/*gentes*, along with the rest of the region, still took advantage of every lull in the action against their joint external enemies to try and gain a bit of extra wealth or an advantage at the cost of another Latin community or clan.

Latin Society in the Fourth Century BC

Both Rome's relationship with the rest of Latium and Latin society itself changed substantially in the first half of the fourth century BC. Looking first at the changes in Latin society, many of the trends which are evident in Rome during this period are also there in the rest of the region, particularly with regards to the settling down of the mobile clans and the rise of more powerful and cohesive communities and city-states. This is visible in the archaeological record via the same markers as at Rome, with the advent of more (and more extensive) city walls, increased evidence for irrigation and agricultural investment at rural villa sites and more substantial structures in and around the communities in general. All of this points to far more permanent associations between clans and communities, along with a stronger sense of community and an increasingly strict delineation between 'us' and 'them'. Unfortunately the literary record thins out for this period, with Livy representing our only complete narrative source for the fourth century BC (although his narrative can be supplemented by anecdotes from Plutarch and others). Given both Livy's focus on Rome and the nature of his evidence, the narrative for events in the rest of Latium is problematic to say the least, but even so this basic model, which saw the rise of powerful, cohesive communities and a decline in the mobility of the region's clans, is generally supported by a number of literary clues. These include the association between clans and particular communities in the narrative and more concerted, cohesive foreign policies by various communities. These developments led to a number of more subtle changes, which would dramatically impact the relationship which existed between the various entities in the region. Perhaps the most important is a decline in the regional homogeneity which had existed previously and the rise of more distinct socio-political and cultural entities. As at Rome, the settling down of the elite clans and their long-term association with particular communities led to the creation of increasingly cohesive and long-lasting aristocracies, like Rome's emerging 'nobility', where individual and clan success was increasingly linked to the overall success of the community. This meant that the region was no longer unified by a fluid and mobile collection of clans, which moved between the communities and effectively maintained equilibrium in the region, but was instead developing a series of powerful and distinct urban centres, dominated by stable aristocracies, each with its own agenda. Alongside these increasingly powerful, but polarizing urban centres there still existed a number of smaller entities (smaller communities, unattached clans and tribes, etc.), although these were increasingly marginalized. The fourth century BC seems to have represented a very different age from that which came before it – everything seemed to be a bit bigger and existed on a grander stage (something which was not only true for Italy, but also for the Greek world).

For Rome's relationship with the Latins, the biggest repercussion of this set of changes was an increasingly divergent foreign policy. While Rome and the rest of the Latins had previously been able to agree on (and fight against) mutual enemies, the fourth century BC saw the region begin to split in this regard. Rome, still reeling from the Gallic sack and being the furthest north of the major Latin settlements – not to mention sitting across the main access point in the north of the region – was fixated on the Gallic threat. As argued above, the sack of the city had sparked major changes within Rome's social and political systems and it is clear that the city was interested in mobilizing the rest of the region against this enemy. However, the southern portion of Latium had its own problems, most notably with the Samnites. A tribal people from south-central Italy, the Samnites had been part of the wider wave of migrations in the mid- to late fifth century BC from the interior towards the western coastal plains. While the Aequi and the Volsci had seen limited success in northern Latium, these tribal peoples had had a little more success further south, with the Volsci evidently capturing and settling in the region of Satricum and the Samnites moving into northern Campania and southern Latium. As a result, the Latins in southern Latium were far more interested in defending against this threat than protecting Rome and the north of the region from the occasional incursion by roving Gauls. Add to this an evident worry about Rome's increasingly imperialist tendencies, as the city had started to acquire more and more land as opposed to simply raiding for portable wealth as she had done before, and there seems to have been a general breakdown in the (albeit limited) regional cohesion which had existed before. Without powerful clans moving between the communities of Latium, interests began to become much more localized and specific to the increasingly defined populations of the various communities.

Many scholars have puzzled over this period and Rome's evidently changing relationship with the Latins. It is clear, both from the later events of the 340s BC and the series of wars fought during the early decades of the fourth century BC, that the situation and set of relationships in Latium were both dynamic and fluid – but their development is not entirely logical, particularly if the reader comes in with the understanding that Rome and the Latins had consistent foreign policies during this period. They are sometimes allied, sometimes at war and sometimes indifferent spectators during the fourth century BC, and there is little in the evidence to explain why they changed positions so quickly and readily. Some have argued that the *foedus Cassianum* had perhaps expired by this point and that the Latin League may have been effectively defunct (although the sources do suggest they were still meeting and electing dictators). And while 'expired' may be the wrong word to apply to this situation with the *foedus Cassianum*, this sort of interpretation does seem to explain the chaos which is evident in Latium's relationships at this time – the rules which had governed relationships in Latium previously, however little they were actually followed in the fifth century BC, seem to have been thrown out of the window in the fourth century BC.

Without any solid evidence to explain this situation, the standard interpretations have been that the Latins were often rebelling from Rome's rule (although there is no real evidence for Rome's overt rule before) or the previously mentioned possible lapsing of the treaty. Either option is naturally possible, although neither is entirely satisfactory given the likely anachronistic nature of the bilateral interpretation of the *foedus* or the full picture of Rome and Latium's development during this period. A far simpler answer might be that the society, and group of entities, which signed up to the *foedus Cassianum* in the early fifth century BC were no longer around in the middle of the fourth century BC; that, far from expiring or lapsing, the treaty was imply no longer appropriate.

Latin society in the early fifth century BC, just like that in Rome at the same time, was still dominated by powerful, mobile clans. As a result, it is probable that both the *foedus Cassianum* and the Latin League itself were based on the relationships which existed between the region's powerful clans and the emerging urban centres. This can arguably be seen by the nature and location of the meeting of the league, at the festival of *Jupitar Latiaris* at Lucus Ferentinae – the highest peak in the Alban Hills – and not at a community or more civic space. This meeting, in addition to including the official business of the league, was also for conducting marriages between clans and settling grievances. As a result, while it is entirely possible (and indeed likely) that communities also sent representatives to this meeting, the annual meeting of the Latin League seems to have been, at its core, a time for the region's clans to get together on neutral territory, with a ritual ban on conflict, to sort out their differences and agree on any possible joint measures for the future. As our few recorded anecdotes about the meeting indicate (unfortunately all from the Regal period), the interactions which took place were most likely personal in nature. The meeting, and probably the league, seems to have been primarily about securing interests for the Latin clans and their leaders, which were quite fluid. The *foedus Cassianum* may have therefore represented an attempt to set down a few basic rules in the early fifth century BC, as both the clans and the communities found themselves increasingly under pressure from tribes like the Aequi and Volsci. It established the basics of the 'Latin rights', which allowed the continued mobility of the clans between communities, along with a system for concerted action against an outside threat. Indeed, the use of a dictator and the system of command for the Latin army, from what we can tell, reassembles Rome's own compromise with her local clans regarding military leadership – although this may be more because of historigraphical issues than reality. However, the system as it existed in the fifth century BC should probably be viewed in the same way as other gentilicial agreements – more like a set of guidelines (albeit backed by both cultural and ritual aspects) than absolute rules. It established some basic structures, but as the groups involved remained reasonably fluid and moved about the region (and indeed some evidently left the region while others moved into it), it was not a rigid treaty per se. So although Dionysius and the later Romans seem to have interpreted it as a mutual defence agreement between the thirty *prisci Latini*, in reality it seems to have simply represented little more than an acknowledgement of the shared interests and rights of those who lived in Latium. It appears to be a flexible arrangement and system which could be used when appropriate, but which was not necessarily binding or required if a group's interests were not in line with the rest. And while the course of the fifth century BC saw these shared interests buffeted and battered, as the region's burgeoning communities started to assert their dominance, the fourth century BC saw them completely torn asunder. The rise to power of distinct polities in Latium and the decline in mobility of the clans meant that there was no longer an easily identifiable set of interests shared by all the Latins, or even a majority. Instead, there were multiple sets which were championed by various groups – Rome pushing for defence against the Gauls, southern Latium urging defence against the Samnites and an increasing number of Latins pushing back against Rome's increasingly aggressive expansion.

The result of this changing dynamic is the very odd relationship which seemed to exist between Rome and the Latins during the fourth century BC. A region which was once (at least loosely) unified by a fluid collection of clans, a way of life and clear external enemies, was now a collection of polities which appeared to have formed their own subset of alliances based on more localized interests. So although they still shared a common language and culture, and indeed still seem to have gone through the motions of the league, the real energy and meaning behind it had disappeared. With this model in place, the changes within the region's internal politics and dynamics start to come into focus, with different communities and groups of communities pushing for their interests, sometimes with and sometimes against communities like Rome. This multi-faceted relationship also helps to explain Rome's response after the Latin War of 340–338 BC (which we will address subsequently), when she seems to treat groups of Latin communities and tribes in very different ways – offering some of them citizenship while punishing others harshly. So for the most part, the fourth century BC can be seen as a period of political fragmentation within Latium – something which, perhaps ironically, was only stopped by the Latins' increasing animosity towards and fear of Rome in the middle of the century.

Colonization and Rome's Early Navy

In this period of political fragmentation amongst the Latins, marked by the rise of more powerful and cohesive polities, we also have some very intriguing developments in the area of colonization. As noted previously, early Roman colonization probably resembled the Greek practice in many ways. This was not because the Italian practice was in any way based on the Hellenistic model. In fact, the Italians had most likely been founding colonies before the Greeks arrived in the early Iron Age. There is a long tradition of Italic tribes, when their population reached a critical amount, splintering off to form new groups and settlements. This was sometimes accomplished with the splinter group sighting and following a particular animal, often a boar or a wolf, until the animal settled down, and then founding the new settlement at that location. This practice was naturally laden with ritual and religious connotations, but was also incredibly practical as the locations where these animals settled down were usually well away from existing populations and contained the basics needed for a small settlement, including food and water. This practice naturally became more formal and sophisticated as time went on, but the basic system of forming new colonies in order to keep a population within the carrying capacity of the land was one with which the Romans and Latins were very familiar. As with Greek colonies, these new settlements usually became entirely independent after they were founded, although they often maintained sentimental links with their mother community, in addition to the very real bonds of kinship and blood. Despite the anachronistic assertions of Rome's late Republican historians, who viewed all colonization through the lens of 'empire', this more independent type of colonization probably typified the Roman practice during the Regal and early Republican periods. As a result, the concept of Roman or Latin colonies during this period is arguably inapplicable. Although possibly founded by Roman or Latin populations, or indeed jointly, the colonies would have effectively become new Latin settlements (based solely on culture and language) once they were founded, and would not have owed any real allegiance to their mother communities. Although there seems to have been a rough sense of Latin identity, there was no such thing as Latin 'citizenship' (and even Roman citizenship is problematic), even in the middle of the fifth century BC – 'Latin Rights' being likely based on cultural identity and not political affiliation. As a result, early colonization seems to have had the same fluid character as much of the rest of Latin society during this time.

With the advent of the fourth century BC and the rise of more cohesive urban polities, it seems that the community of Rome recognized that the old way of colonizing was no longer in the city's best interests. The needs which drove colonization in the Archaic period were naturally still there. Rome had to be very careful that her population did not exceed the carrying capacity of the land around the community and indeed it is likely that she was pulling more and more resources from further and further afield in order to feed her growing citizen body. Additionally, the literary sources and archaeology are unanimous in suggesting a growing desire for and exploitation of land by the Romans in the fourth century BC. As already argued, this is one of the reasons behind Rome's increasing bellicosity during the period, but it is likely that it would also have led to an increased desire to found new colonies – as this represented the traditional, and by far the easiest, mechanism for acquiring new land for poorer citizens. However, colonization would have also served to weaken Rome, taking citizens away from the community and spreading them across new lands, right when she was desperately attempting to increase her manpower reserves. As a result, as suggested in the previous chapter, although Rome founded four new colonies (Satricum, Sutrium, Nepete and Setia) in the 380s BC, she did not create any further colonies for an entire generation. Instead, Rome attempted a number of new ways to deal with this situation, including the creation of *municipia*, like that at Tusculum, and the increased use of *ager publicus*. It was only in the final decades of the fourth century BC that Rome returned to colonization as a viable option, when the city founded a series of new colonies along the coast. It is clear from the nature of these new colonies, however, that things had definitely changed during the intervening years. While Rome's earlier colonies seem to have been independent, and indeed even the late foundation at Satricum (founded in the 380s BC) evidently had to be recaptured in 346 BC, these new colonies were 'full citizen colonies' and extensions of Roman military might. The colonists at these new foundations, dubbed *coloniae maritimae* (maritime colonies), all explicitly retained their Roman citizenship and association. Although limited in size, with only 300 initial colonists, these new foundations were also planned as part of a new, larger military strategy. This can be seen through their grant of *sacrosancta vacatio militia*, a military exemption supposedly held by all members of the *coloniae maritimae* which required them to stay on site at the colony but, evidently in recognition of their importance in guarding the coastline, exempted them from normal military obligations and duties. Between 340 and 240 BC, Rome founded ten of these colonies down the west coast of Italy (Ostia, Antium, Tarracina, Minturnae, Sinuessa, Sena Gallica, Castrum Novum, Pyrgi, Alsium and Fregenae) as part of a concerted pattern of expansion aimed at controlling the sea.

Rome's apparent interest in naval affairs during this period might strike the casual observer as a bit odd. After all, Rome was supposedly a novice in naval combat in the First Punic War (264 to 241 BC), without a ship of her own and entirely reliant on her allies' navies until stolen Carthaginian naval technology (the fortuitous wreck of a Carthaginian trireme which gave the Romans the plans for their construction) allowed the creation of her own fleet. Or at least that is the traditional narrative. There are some slight discrepancies to this story, however. The creation of the *coloniae maritimae* clearly signals an increased interest in at least controlling the coast from the late fourth century BC, although this was done from the land in what might be considered a more traditional Roman approach. Linked to this interest, however, was the creation in 311 BC of the *duovir navalis*, a team of two magistrates tasked with buying or building ships and conducting naval operations. This indicates that, contrary to the generally accepted narrative, Rome did in fact have at least a nascent navy active in the late fourth century BC, almost fifty years before the First Punic War. In fact the sources record that one of these new naval magistrates was active the year after the office's creation, raiding near the Bay of Naples in 310 BC. So the Romans seem to have had a navy of their own from at least 310 BC, although how this is reconciled with Polybius' claim that the Romans did not build their own ships until the 260s BC is uncertain. It is possible that the Romans actually purchased their ships in this early period, thus making Polybius technically correct in that they did not build them, or perhaps they utilized the more common, multipurpose ships during this time and did not have custom-built warships until the 260s BC.

The advent of Rome's navy and the *coloniae maritimae* not only suggests that Rome's interests were expanding beyond the confines of Central Italy and towards the Mediterranean more generally, but also an increasing strategic awareness and both the foresight and ability to invest in military infrastructure. The creation of both the *coloniae maritimae* and a fleet required a form of delayed gratification on the part of the Romans. With regards to the *coloniae*, despite the Romans' evident desire to increase their military manpower during the fourth century BC, they granted the colonists sent to these new foundations an official exemption from service – provided that they maintained Rome's naval security at these new coastal locations. This hints that the Romans recognized that the long-term control of the coast was a benefit which outweighed the short-term boost in manpower which these colonists would have provided. The creation of a fleet represents an even more extreme example of this. Roman warfare was generally a rather inexpensive enterprise; it was primarily about acquiring portable wealth as opposed to spending it. In the fifth and fourth centuries BC, Roman soldiers would supply their own equipment and often their own supplies, with some of this cost being offset by the *stipendium* collected from the populace. The army would then venture out, acquire wealth via either raiding or conquest in the fourth century BC, and then return home at the end of the campaigning season. The only costs for the community as a whole was therefore the *stipendium*, which was both limited and irregular. Instead, it was generally assumed that any costs of warfare incurred by the army would be taken out of the spoils of war, and the *stipendium* was supposed to have been refunded out of these – although how often this actually happened is debated. Indeed, the reason Roman soldiers fought during this period was unlikely to have been from either a sense of proto-nationalism or duty, or because of the limited *stipendium*, but rather from the desire for booty and spoils – this was the main motivator. Warfare was therefore something which occurred largely out of the civic sphere. The generals were elected by the community and the soldiers were associated with Rome, either as citizens or allies, and of course there was a *stipendium* available in case the war was unsuccessful or did not recoup its expenses. But once the army was in the field, it existed as a discrete and separate entity from the urban city of Rome and was generally supposed to earn its own keep. Navies, however, were very different creatures – particularly by the fourth century BC.

The earliest ancient navies, both in Italy and elsewhere in the Mediterranean, seem to have followed roughly the same model as

Rome's early armies. In a time of need, wealthy individuals would lend their ships (and likely their crews) to the community for use in war. Many of these ships, although primarily used for trade, were eminently serviceable as warships as well – as noted before, the difference between an ancient merchant and an ancient pirate was often simply a question of opportunity. So although they were not custom-built for war, they could easily handle a complement of soldiers and were reasonably manoeuvrable and effective fighting platforms. From the seventh and sixth centuries BC, there was an incremental move in the eastern Mediterranean toward more purpose-built warships, most notably triremes (named because of their three banks of oars), although the cost and single function limited their popularity. Although triremes were incredibly effective in military situations, being far faster and more manoeuvrable than the multipurpose ships utilized before, it was hard to convince the wealthy citizens to invest in them. To build, equip, and staff one trireme seems to have cost between 10,000 and 12,000 drachmas, which was a significant outlay. While a multipurpose ship could be used for trade and other activities when the community was not at war, a trireme was suited for no other purpose and had to be carefully maintained (kept out of water in a ship shed) in order to maintain its seaworthiness. These ships were the high-end sports cars of their day – expensive luxury items which were not suited for everyday use. During the fifth century BC, however, the rise of the powerful Greek navies (like that of the Athenians) and the wars against the Persians changed the equation. In conflicts with these types of enemies, the old-fashioned, multipurpose ships were simply outclassed, although they did continue to play a role, and triremes were a 'must-have' item if one wanted to compete. As a result, communities like Athens and others around Greece poured immense amounts of state money into their navies – investing heavily in this technology. Moving away from privately-funded initiatives, Greek states built hundreds of triremes and their associated ship sheds, in addition to spending huge amounts on the salaries of rowers – in the case of Athens, effectively creating an entirely new class of citizen. This development turned warfare, or at least naval warfare, into an almost entirely state-based, state-centred activity. This would, eventually, have a knock-on effect on land warfare, which became increasingly mercenary in nature and which ultimately, by the fourth century BC, had also become effectively a state expenditure with the rise of professional and mercenary armies like those of Philip II and Alexander the Great of Macedon. This was the world of naval warfare into which Rome was venturing in the late fourth century BC – a world of highly professional and specialized fleets which required an enormous 'buy in' from the state in order to simply participate. Given this situation, it is no surprise that Rome took so long to get involved and, even once the city did, was not completely sold on the idea. The requirements of naval warfare went against many of the basic premises which underpinned Roman warfare to that point.

But in the late fourth century BC, Rome did slowly invest in naval infrastructure. Although the details are hazy to say the least, Rome's *duoviri navalis* evidently acquired ships and were active in raids up and down the coast of Italy. So, although it represents an arguably minor and often ignored aspect of Roman warfare, it actually represents a significant turning point in Rome's approach to war. It suggests that Rome was willing to invest a significant amount of state money, something which was limited given the absence of taxation at this time, in order to buy and maintain ships as part of a larger strategic plan. When this is combined with the contemporary construction of the *Via Appia* (Appian Way), a military road designed to move Rome's armies south faster and more effectively, an entirely new phase in Roman warfare seems to have dawned. Gone were the days when warfare was expected to pay for itself, an activity which occurred largely outside of the state's concern, and instead there existed a mindset where Rome was willing and able to invest state resources in military infrastructure to encourage and allow long-term success. Rome seems to have finally entered an era of truly state-based warfare.

The Latin War and the Settlement of 338 BC

The rise of Rome as a cohesive state in both political and military terms, along with the increasingly disparate goals and interests of the various Latin communities, ultimately led to the 'Latin War' of 340–338 BC. Livy offers a rather confusing account of the origins of this conflict, which revolved around the very odd relationship which seems to have existed between Rome, the rest of the Latins, the Samnites and various other local tribes like the Sidicini. According to the narrative, in 341 BC the Romans signed a treaty with the Samnites to end the First Samnite War, which may have represented a renewal of an agreement set in 354 BC. Rome had evidently been a slightly unwilling participant in this war, despite her reasonable success in it, having been dragged in by the Campanians. The people of Campania, and the city of Capua in particular, had come to Rome asking for help against the Samnites in 343 BC. Rome had initially refused this request, noting that they already held a treaty with the Samnites, until the Campanians fully surrendered themselves (*deditio*) to the Romans – throwing themselves on their mercy. This ploy evidently worked and the Romans took up the war of the Campanians against the Samnites, winning a number of victories, although they seemed quite happy to sign a treaty in 341 BC in order to extricate themselves from the situation. The Samnites had apparently been more interested in the land of the Sidicini, an Oscan people who lived in Campania, than anything else and were happy to leave Rome's new Campanian allies/ subjects alone. Despite this fact, Rome's peace treaty did not sit well with the Campanians, who were still worried about the Samnite threat, and it most definitely did not appeal to the Sidicini, who were now the main focus of Samnite aggression. These two groups then allied with some of the Latins against Rome, the Campanians citing a Roman betrayal and playing on the existing fears in Latium of Rome's rising power. The subsequent conflict between Rome and the various allies was decidedly lopsided with Rome winning five quick victories between 340 and 338 BC (at the Veseris River, Trifanum, Fenectane Plains, Pedum and the

Astura River) against a set of haphazardly assembled allied armies. The end result was Rome's complete victory over the region and a complete reinterpretation of relationships between the various communities.

The sequence of events and motivations surrounding both the First Samnite War and the 'Great' Latin War are both complex and confusing, and many scholars have argued that much of the narrative was probably invented by either Livy or his sources. The surrender or *deditio* of the Campanians, for instance, is often argued to be a fabrication in order to explain why the Romans seem to have broken the treaty of 354 BC with the Samnites, while Livy's narrative for the start of the Latin War is full of speeches and propaganda that could not possibly have been preserved from the time itself (the first speech which was supposedly written down in Rome is dated to several decades later). As a result, modern scholarship has generally settled on the position that while the wars themselves most likely happened, and the end result (Rome's victory) seems clear, the exact 'how' and 'why' may be beyond us given the nature of the evidence. In particular, the various relationships at play simply do not seem to make sense. Rome's relationship with the Samnites will be discussed in detail in the next chapter, but it has often puzzled scholars how the Romans could move from being at war with the Samnites in 341 BC, to supposedly being allied to the Samnites the very next year in the war against the Latins (although the role played by the Samnites in this conflict is also quite contentious). Alternatively, why would the Campanians, who were evidently in such a weak position in 343 BC that they fully surrendered to Rome, try to attack both Rome and the Samnites together only two years later? An alliance with some of the Latins and other tribes would have probably helped, but it is doubtful whether this would have been enough to give them a chance in such a war, as the end result clearly showed.

The one relationship which does seem clear is that which existed between Rome and the Latins. The sources are unanimous on the fact that the Campanians were able to convince a number of local Latin communities, who were also worried about the Samnite threat to the south and Rome's growing power to the north, to join their war against Rome. Although the result, an ignominious defeat, makes the decision on the part of the Latins seem foolhardy in retrospect, it makes quite a bit of sense given recent developments in Latium and the increasingly fractured approach to foreign policy in the region. Many of the Latin communities in the south would have felt they had much more in common with the Campanian communities, which were also major trading partners, than with Rome – despite the shared language and culture. Indeed, the alliance also seems to have included the Volsci, who had settled near the community of Satricum, suggesting it should be seen as more of a southern Latium/Campanian regional coalition. This suggests, as already argued, that the rise of distinct polities in Latium in the fourth century BC had effectively broken down any sort of pre-existing regional unity in Latium, which was replaced by more localized interests and ultimately alliances.

Although Livy regularly uses the term 'the Latins' when discussing this war, harking back to the old days of the Latin League, it is likely that not all of the Latins joined the war against the Romans and indeed it probably included only the southern communities (Trifanum, Pedum, Manuvium, Aricia and Velitrae are mentioned by Livy). The result, however, did ultimately have an impact upon the entire region. After the war, the Romans evidently went around the region of Latium, setting up discrete settlements/alliances with each Latin community which seem to have reflected the very individual relationship which Rome had with each one. Communities which had been actively involved in the war, including Lanuvium, Aricia, Nomentum and Pedum, were transformed into *municipia* and, along with the old *municipium* of Tusculum, assigned to Roman tribes. This direct incorporation may seem a little odd, given their opposition to Rome, although it may reflect Rome's acknowledgement of the strength of these communities and a desire to make their resources and manpower her own (or, perhaps, it simply represented the best way to keep them in check). The treatment of Tibur and Praeneste, which represented the most powerful communities in Latium outside of Rome, was different as, although they were forced to cede territory to Rome, they maintained their independence and effectively became dependent satellites of Rome, both communities giving up all foreign policy decisions to the Roman senate. The rest of Latium seems to have continued as before with most communities keeping their existing political structures, although it is probable that foreign relations were affected by the sudden regional shift in power which occurred after 338 BC. Captured Volscian and Campanian communities were all treated slightly differently. At Velitrae, for instance, the Volscian aristocracy was evidently forced into exile, the walls of the settlement were removed and land distributed to new Roman colonists. Campanian communities such as Capua largely escaped the harsh treatment meted out to the Volsci, and were generally incorporated into the Roman state as *municipia* like the Latin communities involved in the war.

The impact of the Latin War and the subsequent settlement was profound for Roman warfare and the Roman approach to conquest. Although the Romans of the late Republic seem to have viewed this event as an uprising or rebellion, with the post-338 BC environment a return to a somewhat more secure status quo, many modern scholars have increasingly argued that the year 338 BC and the incorporation of the Latins represented a significant turning point in the history of Rome, if only in that it marked the culmination of Rome's revival after the Gallic sack and the beginning of her wider dominance of Italy. The relationships put in place in 338 BC secured and regularized Rome's relationship with most of the Latin communities, recognizing the changing political landscape of the fourth century BC and replacing the now outdated Latin League with a new federation of communities. It gave Rome effective control over all of *Latium Vetus*, *Latium Adjectum* and Campania, removing almost all of her traditional threats to the south – although opening up a new tension with the Samnites. But more importantly for the present study, the creation of so many *municipia* increased Rome's citizen body exponentially. This new and vast supply of manpower, coupled with a series of alliances, allowed Rome's army to function on an entirely new scale rivalled only by the major Hellenistic powers.

Conclusion

The fourth century BC marked a major turning point in Rome's relationship with the Latins. All of the developments of the previous century, including the rise of more cohesive polities/communities, the decline of the region's mobile clans/*gentes*, the increased importance of land and agriculture and the arrival of the Gauls, served to break apart any regional unity which had previously existed and created new, more localized divisions. Rome and the Latins still shared a culture and a language, but they no longer shared a single vision for regional security. Rome, in the north, found herself increasingly in opposition to the communities in the south of Latium, who seem to have viewed the Samnites (and perhaps Rome herself) as a far greater threat than the Gauls. Each community in Latium seems to have developed its own distinct identity, which led to an increasingly fractured and factionalized region and ultimately resulted in a final war between Rome and those Latin communities who felt most threatened by her rise to power, generally those located in the southern half of the region. Rome's victory over these communities, and the resultant settlement of 338 BC, allowed for a reinterpretation of the relationships in Latium which took into account the changing political situation. Rome emerged as the undisputed master of Central Italy and had at her disposal a huge reserve of manpower through the creation of a number of *municpia* as well as a series of alliances.

This situation changed the Roman army forever. First, it gave Rome a reserve of men which allowed the city to compete with the major Hellenistic powers around the Mediterranean. Without the settlement of 338 BC, Rome would have probably never defeated the Samnites in the final decades of the fourth century BC, let alone a force like that led by Pyrrhus in the early third century BC. The creation of so many new citizens, albeit most of them without voting rights, gave Rome the resources to fight in major conflicts and to come back from defeats time and again. Second, the fourth century BC and the rise of cohesive polities in Latium, most notably at Rome itself, allowed greater strategic vision and planning. With more cohesive communities came the ability and motivation to invest in military infrastructure – roads, colonies and navies. This type of expenditure would have been unthinkable under the more flexible model of the fifth century BC, where Rome's leaders and Roman warfare seems to have had only an ephemeral connection to the city. But with the rise of a Roman nobility, which maintained links to the community for generations, and an increasing realization by the community that warfare could benefit everyone and not just the soldiers involved – generally through the creation and use of *ager publicus* – war became a community endeavour. Finally, the settlement of 338 BC and Rome's conquest of Central Italy created a situation where continued conquest and warfare was almost unavoidable. While the principle of 'defensive imperialism' as the main cause of Rome's expansion has been rightly criticised by scholars such as W.V. Harris and Nathan Rosenstein, Rome's new position in Central Italy did make conflict likely. Rome's involvement in Campania had already drawn her into conflict with the Samnites and this would continue for another fifty years. Rome was also increasingly involved with the Greek communities of Magna Graecia, which would ultimately lead to the arrival of Pyrrhus. So while Rome might not have been an entirely reluctant and defensive conqueror, the city also had quite a few new borders and interests to protect.

Chapter 6

Rome and the Mediterranean World

The previous five chapters have focused predominantly on Rome's relationship with her closest neighbours in Central Italy and how the city gradually emerged as the most dominant military and political power in the region. This was a long process, which had as much to do with Rome's internal political and civic development as it did with Rome's external military success (although obviously the two are related), and the city's resultant supremacy could arguably be seen as a triumph of the community's increasingly single-minded determination against the diverse interests of the Latins. This chapter, however, deals with a rather different set of relationships and Rome's arrival on the wider Mediterranean scene. But while it will chronicle the 'birth of empire' and Rome's varied approach to a range of new peoples and stimuli, many of the same themes which defined Rome's rise to power are still visible. While the late fourth and third centuries BC saw Rome's armies and envoys venturing further and further afield, for increasingly diverse reasons and interests, the core themes of integration and a developing civic identity are still evident and arguably still driving much of Rome's military expansion and development.

Rome's wars during this period, from the mid-fourth century to the mid-third century BC, have been the subject of intense study and debate – particularly during the past fifty years. Beginning with Rome's great conflict with the Samnites (most notably the Second Samnite War or The Great Samnite War), and followed by Rome's war against Pyrrhus and the first conflict with the Carthaginians, the city's foreign interactions during this period were influenced heavily by her new alliance structures and her purported desire to defend the interests of her allies against foreign enemies. Rome's histories for this period are therefore often framed in terms of a 'defensive imperialism', where Rome is portrayed as the reluctant conqueror – being dragged into war after war by her allies, arguably against her will or in pursuit of a greater strategic security. These wars are therefore seen as *iura bella* ('just wars'), or defensive wars, although once Rome became involved in a conflict, however reluctantly, the city pursued it to the end – throwing the entirety of her resources into it. It was this dedication to warfare on the part of the Romans, the ability and determination to return to the battlefield time and again after defeats to Pyrrhus or to build a fleet from scratch in order to engage with the Carthaginians, which is often thought to be the secret to their success in this period. That, and an increasingly evolved army which learned from and adapted to each enemy it fought. Or at least this is what the Romans later claimed.

This simple motif of Rome as the reluctant conqueror has rightly been challenged in recent decades, with W.V. Harris and more recently Nathan Rosenstein both presenting the case for Rome being anything but an unwilling or unenthusiastic participant when it came to war.[1] Warfare formed an important part of elite identity going back to the early Iron Age, and Rome's aristocracy – although increasingly sophisticated and urban – retained a strong martial character throughout the Republican period. However, the tension between the Roman elite's desire to engage in warfare for personal reasons and the evident awkwardness and unpreparedness which seems to have marked the city's approach in the aftermath of this warfare has generally defied a single explanation. Rome's apparently *ad hoc* approach to empire in the middle Republic suggests that a grand strategy was lacking during this period. But at the core of Rome's foreign interactions, underpinning her reaction and response to the requests of her allies and driving the ambitions of her elite, were a set of cultural principles with their origins back in the Archaic period. As a result, although this period clearly represents a new stage and period in Roman warfare and the development of empire, it also needs to be understood as a continuation of previous practices and the result of the same forces which led to Rome's consolidation and her domination over the Latins. The present chapter will endeavour to lay out some of these principles (although a full treatment would require an entire volume – indeed perhaps several! – on its own).

Our understanding of the development of the Roman army as a fighting body, and as a social and cultural institution, has also been revised in recent years. The nature and characteristics of the Roman army during this period have been a subject of interest since the time of Livy, as this period marks the first time that the surviving literary accounts offer anything which resembles a real description of battlefield tactics and organization (Livy 8.8, discussed in detail later, being the most obvious example). This period is therefore generally recognized as the point of origin for not only Rome's territorial empire, but also the Roman army which won it – the so-called manipular legion – although what made the Roman army so different during this period is sometimes hard to determine. Rome's historians all held that the Roman army, at its core, had remained remarkably stable and static during the Republic. The Servian Constitution, supposedly set out in the late Regal period, created the wealth and age-based framework whereby Rome's population was divided up, equipped and organized into a civic militia. While many superficial details changed during the following centuries (most notably the equipment), and sometimes quite quickly, the core principles which underpinned the army were thought to have remained roughly the same. What made the army so successful was therefore thought to be the way in which it changed its superficial aspects – its equipment, formation and tactics – in response to different enemies and situations. And as Rome faced off against more and stronger opponents during the late fourth and third centuries BC, these enemies were thought to have shaped the Roman army – like a whetstone on a sword edge – into the supreme fighting force which ultimately conquered the entirety of the Mediterranean world. However, this development narrative has been slowly revised as the major changes which are evident in Roman society during the sixth, fifth and fourth centuries BC have also been applied to the army, and as military change is more clearly understood. It was once thought, based on military models produced during the Enlightenment, that armies acted rationally and could change their tactics and equipment as easily as one might change a set of clothing. However, an increasing body of sociological and anthropological work has revealed that these types of superficial changes are subject to the same social and cultural rules which govern other aspects of society – and indeed these rules are arguably more important in the sphere of warfare. Military changes very rarely occur in response to the simple arrival of a new technology or approach, but are instead dictated by a range of principles which actually favour conservatism over innovation.[2] The emergence of the manipular legion of the fourth century BC, although most likely a response to new stimuli, was therefore also probably part of a much longer sequence of development in Rome.

Samnite Wars

Rome's empire arguably began with the Samnites. Though the Romans had increasingly extended their power and influence during the fifth century and first half of the fourth century BC, conquering and integrating various Latin peoples and even the Etruscan city of Veii, the extent of her territorial empire was limited. It was really only with the Samnite wars that Rome's reach began to extend beyond the immediate confines of Latium and southern Etruria, grasping at the wealthy Greek communities of Campania and the south. So the Samnites and the Samnite wars represent a key moment of transition for Rome, and the beginnings of an outward push. Additionally, although the Gauls seem to have had the largest impact on Rome's psyche during the fourth century BC, in large part because of the Gallic sack of Rome, Rome's wars against the Samnites seem to have been the greatest test of her army.

The Gallic assault at the River Allia, while not a complete surprise or ambush, still seems to have caught the Romans somewhat unprepared as the army is recorded as fleeing almost immediately in the face of the Gallic charge. However, while every subsequent battle against the Gauls was seen as a major engagement (and the spectre of Allia was evidently always in the back of the Roman mind), the Romans seem to have fared quite well against the Gauls during the rest of the century. The Samnites, on the other hand, seem to have regularly tested the Roman army and, even after Rome's victory in the Third Samnite War, remained a dormant but very real threat until the Social War of the first century BC, where the Samnites once again played a significant role.

The First Samnite War, which lasted from 343 to 341 BC, was a reasonably minor undertaking in the grand scheme of things. The conflict arose out of Rome's increasing involvement in southern Italy, and particularly the region of Campania (which bordered Latium to the south), as part of her general expansion during the course of the fourth century BC. As Rome slowly expanded her interest and influence amongst the communities of Latium, she integrated and incorporated many of their existing interests and associations – which included connections with the south. So although Rome may have had only a passing interest in the region previously, through her allies (and particularly those communities located in southern Latium, like Satricum), the rich communities of southern Italy gradually took on a new meaning and importance. This region, however, was already the focus of a number of groups. Campania had a native population of Oscan-speaking Italians, but had also been settled by the Greeks as early as the eighth century BC with a number of major colonies (including Cumae and Neapolis – modern day Naples) and was increasingly under threat from the Samnites, who had been venturing down to the rich coastal regions from the mountainous areas of south-central Italy since the middle of the fifth century BC. As a result, the region was both divided and already in a state of almost constant low-level warfare, offering an ideal situation for an expansionist Rome to get involved.

The Samnites are an enigmatic people as our only literary descriptions of them were written by outsiders (and enemies) like the Romans, often centuries after they had been incorporated into the Roman state. As a result, ancient authors often seem to have relied on Samnite stereotypes or tropes when describing them, or simply used the Samnites of their own day as a model (for instance, the equipment associated with the Samnites in the fourth century BC seems to have been drawn directly from the Samnite-style gladiators popular during the late Republic). Despite these issues, a few basic aspects of archaic Samnite culture are increasingly clear from a combination of more critical readings of the literature and, more importantly, the available archaeological evidence. The Samnites seem to have been a tribal people who did not have cities or major urban centres themselves. Instead they favoured small, fortified sites on top of centrally-located hills – the famous hillforts of Samnium – which probably served as refuges for tribes which lived and worked in farms located in the valleys below. But although they did not build cities themselves – as the mountainous region of Samnium was decidedly ill-suited to them – they seem to have increasingly realized the wealth and potential which lay in Italy's growing urban centres and, following the general trend for migrations from the Apennine Mountains down to the coastal plains of western Italy which marked the fifth century BC, the Samnites increasingly ventured down into Campania. But while Rome's rise to power, coupled with the strength of the Latins, seem to have put a halt to the progress of similar mountain tribes like the Aequi and Volsci in Latium by the late fifth century BC, the Samnites – either because they were stronger or their opponents were weaker – were able to continue to gain ground in Campania well into the fourth century BC.

The Samnites were not always enemies of Rome. In fact, Rome and the Samnites seem to have had a reasonable working relationship during the early fourth century BC – and even an alliance of sorts – with each accepting and respecting the other's sphere of influence. Rome was only drawn into conflict with the Samnites by her new alliance network when a group of Samnites attacked the Sidicini, a small tribe in northern Campania.[3] The Sidicini themselves were not allies of Rome. They were a tribal people living in northern Campania who, probably realizing that they most likely did not stand a chance against the Samnites alone, asked the people of Campania for assistance – and particularly the major Greek colonies located there – as the Samnites represented a common enemy. The Campanian Greeks agreed and marched out to war, only to be soundly defeated, leaving the Samnites free to push even further into the region. The Samnites very quickly overran the Sidicini and turned their attention to the rich colony of Capua, winning a couple of significant engagements and forcing the citizens of Capua to retreat behind their walls. The Campanians (and particularly the besieged people of Capua) were now very much on the back foot and quickly looked around for allies of their own, and the emerging power of Rome to the north seems to have represented the most viable (and perhaps the least threatening) option. While the Greek communities of Campania may have been wary of involving the Greeks of Apulia or elsewhere in southern Italy in the conflict, perhaps for fear of upsetting the delicate balance of power which existed between them, the Romans may have seemed a safe choice as they had displayed no previous imperialistic tendencies in addition to representing an increasingly formidable military power. So the Campanians went to Rome asking for help against the Samnites – only to be rebuffed by the Senate, supposedly citing their pre-existing agreement with the Samnites (although scholars have often debated how likely this version of events is). But the Campanians, and specifically the people of Capua, were evidently desperate for help and so returned to the Senate and surrendered themselves completely to Roman power – an act known as *deditio*. This act of subjugation was obviously extreme (and, again, some scholars have wondered if this represents a Roman interpretation, or reinterpretation, of events and not what the Campanians intended) but it was also apparently successful and won over the Senate, who then stepped in to help – initially with emissaries (which were unsuccessful) and then via direct military action. Once war was engaged, however, it was actually quite limited. The Romans were active in 343 BC, with both consuls winning a number of battles against the Samnites, albeit sometimes with heavy losses, but there was no reported activity in 342 BC and the Romans and Samnites negotiated a peace treaty in 341 BC – possibly because both sides had trouble to deal with at home. So the First Samnite War was concluded with only one real season of campaigning and without a decisive victory for either side. This is not to say, however, that the situation in 341 BC was the same as in 343 BC. A key development which emerged from the First Samnite War was that the Romans ended the war with a permanent foothold in Campania and an abiding interest in the region – something which would eventually lead to further tension with the Samnites and ultimately a renewing of the conflict.

Between 341 and 338 BC, the Romans were concerned with Latium and the so-called Latin Uprising or Latin War discussed in the previous chapter. Following this war, however, the city turned its attention south once more. From 338 to 326 BC, the Romans slowly pushed south, planting a number of colonies on the coast (the *coloniae maritimae*) along with a massive expansion of *ager publicus* in the interior. As suggested previously, Rome had spent much of the fourth century BC trying out various approaches for how to deal with the issues of paying off her soldiers and what to do with conquered land. This had involved the foundation of traditional colonies, the creation of *municipia* and finally true citizen colonies. But by the late fourth century BC Rome seems to have settled on a new philosophy when it came to captured territory which seems to have become the Roman *modus operandi* for the next century or more. When Rome conquered a new territory, some of the land was set aside for new colonies but the bulk of it was held communally as *ager publicus* (public land) which could be utilized by all Romans. Access to *ager publicus*, coupled with the *stipendium* (a limited salary for soldiers) and cash donatives paid out by the general at the end of a campaign, seems to have been enough to keep at least most of Rome's soldiers happy while also solving the problem of losing manpower or territory when it came time to paying off her troops at the end of the season. But more importantly, it also meant that Roman warfare increasingly benefited the entire community – and particularly the elite who were quickly able to dominate the *ager publicus* – making warfare an ever more appealing activity, even for those not directly involved. The foundation of citizen colonies on captured land was also vital to this new system, as they served to secure the territory and extend Rome's power across the region. Many of these new colonies were located on the coast and seem to have been intended to protect Rome's budding maritime interests, but a few were also planted in areas which had previously been considered Samnite territory – particularly in the Sacco-Liri River valley – leading to a renewal of the conflict with the Samnites in 326 BC.

The Second Samnite War, or 'The Great Samnite War', lasted over twenty years (326–304 BC) and seems to have been the result of aggressive Roman expansion associated with this new approach to land. Although the Roman sources accuse the Samnites of various nefarious acts leading up to the war (inciting Neapolis to attack Rome's interests in Campania, etc.), the conflict actually seems to have been sparked by Roman belligerence as she continued to push her interests further south. Successful warfare had always benefited the victorious general and his soldiers, but the possibility of creating more *ager publicus* seems to have been increasingly appealing to the Roman *populus*, and particularly the senatorial elite, meaning that warfare and the conquest of new land was now a top priority. Indeed, even the Roman sources, which generally attempt to paint these wars as defensive, cannot completely hide the fact that the war was precipitated by Rome's planting of colonies in Samnite territory and Roman provocation.

The record for the early years of 'The Great Samnite War' are incredibly hazy, although things seem to have generally gone the Romans' way between 326 and 321 BC, as in 321 BC the Samnites reportedly sued for peace. However, Livy reports that the terms put forward by the Romans were incredibly harsh and the Samnites were forced to continue the war. Only weeks later, however, the Romans may have regretted this harshness as in the same season they experienced one of their worst defeats since the sack of Rome by the Gauls – the disaster at the Caudine Forks – which saw an entire Roman army surrounded in a narrow ravine and defeated, with the survivors forced to pass 'under the yoke' by the Samnites. This was followed by several years of relative inactivity, although Livy suggests that the Romans were active in 320 and 319 BC trying to exact revenge for the defeat (many scholars question this, as it seems to represent a bit of Roman revisionism), and it was not until 315 BC that they seem to have fully returned to the offensive. But despite the reprieve and the chance to regroup after the Caudine Forks, the Romans still seem to have struggled against the Samnites and suffered yet another major defeat, this time at Lautulae. To make matters worse, the Samnites were joined by the Etruscans in 311 BC, meaning that the Romans were facing threats to both the north and the south.

At this point in the war, something seems to change in Rome. Despite this precarious position, from 311 BC onward everything seems to have gone the Romans' way. After 311 BC they went on to win a string of victories and eventually forced peace with the Etruscans in 308 BC and the Samnites in 304 BC, ending the war. What happened around 311 BC to allow this change is still unknown, although some scholars have suggested the Roman success in the final years of the war may have been the result of military developments sparked by the defeats – and indeed the Romans themselves seem to remember the Samnite wars as marking a period of military change, as will be discussed in the next section. The Third Samnite War, which lasted from 298 to 290 BC, can be viewed as an extension of the second and it was again started through Rome's alliance with a people (the Lucanians) who asked for help against the Samnites. The Samnites were once more joined by the Etruscans in the north, this time aided by Gauls, although the Romans seem to have had little trouble dealing with both the threats and the war was concluded in 291 BC with Rome the effective master of both southern Etruria and Samnium.

Rome's Manipular Army

The Second Samnite War was the background which Livy, our only major literary source for this period, used to describe the changes in Rome's army during the fourth century BC and the advent of the so-called 'manipular legion'. In the following passage, which is arguably one of the most famous and important relating to Rome's early military development during the Republic, Livy offers a general description of Rome's military development to that time along with one of the most detailed descriptions of Rome's military tactics:

The Romans had formerly used small round shields; then, after they began to serve for pay,[4] they made oblong shields instead of round ones; and what had before been a phalanx, like the Macedonian phalanxes, came afterwards to be a line of battle formed by maniples, with the rearmost troops drawn up in a number of companies. The first line, or *hastati*, comprised fifteen maniples, stationed a short distance apart; the maniple had twenty light-armed soldiers, the rest of their number carried oblong shields; moreover those were called 'light-armed' who carried only a spear and javelins. This front line in the battle contained the flower of the young men who were growing ripe for service. Behind these came a line of the same number of maniples, made up of men of a more stalwart age; these were called the *principes*; they carried oblong shields and were the most showily armed of all. This body of thirty maniples they called *antepilani*, because behind the standards there were again stationed another fifteen companies, each of which had three sections, the first section in every company being known as *pilus*. The company consisted of three *vexilla* or 'banners'; a single *vexillum* had sixty soldiers, two centurions, one *vexillarius*, or colourbearer; the company numbered a hundred and eighty-six men. The first banner led the *triarii*, veteran soldiers of proven valour; the second banner the *rorarii*, younger and less distinguished men; the third banner the *accensi*, who were the least dependable, and were, for that reason, assigned to the rear-most line. When an army had been marshalled in this fashion, the *hastati* were the first of all to engage. If the *hastati* were unable to defeat the enemy, they retreated slowly and were received into the intervals between the companies of the *principes*. The *principes* then took up the fighting and the *hastati* followed them. The *triarii* knelt beneath their banners, with the left leg advanced, having their shields leaning against their shoulders and their spears thrust into the ground and pointing obliquely upwards, as if their battle-line were fortified with a bristling palisade. If the *principes*, too, were unsuccessful in their fight, they fell back slowly from the battle-line on the *triarii*. (From this arose the adage, 'to have come to the *triarii*,' when things are going badly.) The *triarii*, rising up after they had received the *principes* and *hastati* into the intervals between their companies, would at once draw their companies together and close the lanes, as it were; then, with no more reserves behind to count on, they would charge the enemy in one compact array. This was a thing exceedingly disheartening to the enemy, who, pursuing those whom they supposed they had conquered, all at once beheld a new line rising up, with augmented numbers. There were customarily four legions raised of five thousand foot each, with three hundred horse to every legion.[5]

Although Livy seems to suggest that many of the changes he described took place half a century earlier, back in the early fourth century, many scholars have argued that the Samnite wars may have also played a significant role in the development of Rome's equipment and tactics. As the Romans were traditionally thought to have fought in a phalanx

formation, a catalyst or impetus was needed to break apart this formation
into the more flexible and fragmented army which historians, such as
Polybius, describe for the third and second centuries BC. The phalanx
formation had been proven to be incredibly successful across the
Mediterranean, so long as armies were fighting on reasonably level
terrain – like the great coastal plain of Latium. However, moving into the
rugged and mountainous land of south-central Italy where the Samnites
lived would have been problematic for a phalanx, and it was suggested
that this is why the Romans may have struggled in the middle years of
the war. These issues, along with the precarious position in which the
city found itself in 311 BC, might have led to the Romans breaking up
their phalanx into the manipular formation – a loose checkerboard made
up of groups of 120 men of various equipment types. An army broken
up into maniples or *manipuli*, which literally means 'handfuls' in Latin,
would have been able to maintain tactical cohesion across broken terrain
far more easily than a phalanx. Additionally, texts like the *Ineditum
Vaticanum*, which purportedly records an interaction between a Roman
envoy and the Carthaginians before the start of the First Punic War, have
provided fuel for this fire.[6]

As noted in Chapter One, the *Ineditum Vaticanum* records the
Carthaginians asking the Romans why they think they can engage in
a naval war with them when the Romans have no experience of naval
combat, and indeed no fleet. The Romans respond that they have long
excelled by learning from their opponents, adapting to new types of
warfare and borrowing tactics and equipment when it suited them –
becoming 'masters of those who thought so highly of themselves'. This
speech and the idea of the student overcoming the master is quite clearly
a rhetorical trope, although it is one in which the Romans seem to have
believed – at least in the late Republic – as it generally sums up the broad
narrative of military development which we find in other sources as well.
Looking specifically at the manipular legion, this passage suggests that
the Romans acquired oblong shields and javelins – two key pieces of

equipment used by the manipular legion – from the Samnites, furthering the association between the adoption of this formation and this period. Our changing understanding of the Roman army in the fifth and early fourth century BC, however, coupled with some interesting developments in archaeology, has suggested a somewhat messier, but far more organic, sequence of development.

As already suggested, the traditional starting point for the Roman army in the early fourth century – as a civic militia fighting in a hoplite (or possible Macedonian) phalanx formation – has generally been discarded by most modern scholars for a number of very good reasons. As a result, entering the fourth century BC there is no need to search for a reason to 'break up' the phalanx into a more flexible formation, as it is likely that the Roman army – based previously on a collection of disparate clans – already deployed in something resembling a manipular formation. Although they may have stood next to each other on the battle field, Rome's military was probably still organized in small groups (based on either clans or *curiae*), was used to engaging in raiding activities which favoured small flexible groups and so was most likely made up of a number of individual and independent units – or *manipuli* – anyway. The real change in the fourth century BC was therefore not the breaking up of the phalanx, but actually bringing these various units, or *manipuli*, together into a single entity and fighting consistently under a single banner.

The real strength or advantage of Rome's manipular army was not new equipment or tactics per se, although the structure did allow for these, but its ability to include and incorporate a range of different units into a single military structure. This ability to integrate new groups and units seems to have originated within the community of Rome itself, as the Romans needed to have a military system which allowed her clan-based units to fight alongside community-based units, although during the course of the fourth century BC the system was also required to integrate an increasing number of allied units – most notably the Latins, but also, by the late fourth century BC, Greeks. Each of these groups seems to have had their own tactics and style of combat, in addition to different goals and aims, and the Roman system had to be able to accommodate this while still fielding an effective overall fighting force. The result was an incredibly flexible system, particularly in the fourth century BC, where the Roman army would have resembled a patchwork of different units when mobilized on the battlefield: Roman and Latin *gentes*, equipped in their classic equipment; soldiers from the city of Rome itself, likely equipped in newer and perhaps lighter equipment; Campanian horsemen, etc. – all drawn up in their individual groups. Each unit would then go on to fight and act largely independently, utilizing their individual strengths and abilities for often quite personal gains (spoils and booty, acquired in individual combat, were still key), albeit generally working together for a common victory. Indeed, there seems to have been quite a bit of space within the Roman battle line (if this term can even be used), as the sources are full of stories of individuals and war leaders seeking each other out, riding up and down (and sometimes through) the army while it was evidently engaged, even at this late date.

While the Roman army of the fourth century BC seems to have featured a number of different troop types, this sort of open formation would have also made quite a bit of sense given what the archaeology suggests was occurring in terms of military equipment in Central Italy. The region's archaic *gentes* seem to have preferred fighting with large, circular shields (the *aspis* or *hoplon*), heavy body armour and thrusting spears. Although these pieces of equipment became associated with the hoplite phalanx and hoplite warfare in Greece, evidence suggests (as argued convincingly by van Wees, amongst others) that this type of equipment was initially designed to provide optimal protection in individual combat.[7] In fact, once a dense formation is adopted, much of the defensive equipment usually associated with hoplites becomes redundant (the formation providing the bulk of the defence), as seen in the gradual removal of equipment in Greek hoplite armies – when Athens distributes equipment to hoplites for the first time in the late fourth century BC it is just a helmet and shield

– and in the 'enhanced' phalanx deployed in Macedon where the armour is almost entirely removed in favour of a dense formation armed with *sarissae*. It is probable that the archaic Roman and Latin *gentes* continued to equip themselves in this manner in the fourth century BC, in large part because this was the equipment they already owned, and fought in a similar manner on the battlefield.

Romans and Latins who had not regularly participated in warfare previously (or who at least did not have their own equipment) but who wanted to (or were expected to) join the army in the fourth century BC would have had a few more options – and it seems that quite a few adopted a new style of equipment which was increasingly in fashion at the time. Most likely introduced by the Gauls (there is extensive archaeological evidence for this type of equipment in southern Austria and other Gallic regions going back to the late Bronze Age), this equipment featured a handful of javelins and an oblong shield (offering better protection against thrown javelins, particularly for the legs). Far cheaper than the heavy bronze equipment which had been used in the Archaic period by the gentilicial elite, this new panoply was gradually adopted throughout Central Italy during the course of the fourth century BC – and particularly by the Lucanians and Samnites of South-Central Italy. The Roman association between the Samnites and this style of equipment is somewhat fitting then, although it seems as if they were not its point of origin. Instead, the Samnites could possibly be described as 'early adopters' – perhaps because they lacked a strong, alternative tradition of military equipment from the Archaic period. This new reliance on the javelin throughout Central Italy, albeit likely in conjunction with a backup weapon like a sword or axe, would have also encouraged a more open and flexible battle order. Unlike the Roman armies of the late Republic – where it is often thought that the Romans would follow a hail of *pila* with a charge and direct, hand-to-hand combat – the javelin-armed soldiers of the fourth century BC seem to have been far more lightly armed and armoured (if the depictions from tombs at sites like Paestum can be trusted). As a result, it is likely that a battle would have featured several volleys of javelins before more direct battle was eventually engaged – if it ever was. In order to allow as many units, let alone individuals, to throw their javelins as possible (and to avoid hitting allied units) a fairly loose battle order would have made sense – and here some parallels can be drawn from tribes like the Yanomamo in Brazil, which still featured this type of javelin-based warfare (including oblong shields) well into the twentieth century.[8]

The manipular army of the fourth century BC should therefore not be seen as the highly regimented and organized Roman legion described in Livy 8.8, although one can see hints of the truth behind Livy's anachronistic façade. Livy's *velites, hastati, principes, triarii*, etc. are likely the later formalizations of what were originally de facto divisions or troop types; the *triarii* representing the archaic warbands, with their heavy armour and long tradition of warfare, while the other groups represented various cultural, ethnic or merely economic groups, featuring the equipment which they had traditionally utilized or which they could now afford. Amongst these other groups the javelin was clearly key, although they also probably utilized a range of other equipment types and varying levels of armour. Over the course of the fourth and third centuries BC, things were gradually formalized and standardized, and the massive impact of battles like Cannae – where a generation of soldiers and a huge amount of equipment was lost – cannot be overstated, but the army's origins seem to have been far more fluid.

Despite these more organic (and possibly less impressive) origins, the development of the manipular legion in the fourth century BC still represented a major achievement. It should be noted that the ability to effectively combine units of different types, and from a number of different socio-political entities, in a single army was not unknown at this time. Indeed, the army of Philip II and Alexander the Great of Macedon arguably represents another example of this 'combined arms' approach – with the army unified by both the promise of payment and, later, the charisma of the leader. And of course the use of mercenaries in the Greek world more generally in the fifth and fourth centuries BC, particularly with regards to light infantry (*peltasts*), would have offered another example. But what made Rome's manipular army so interesting and effective was its ability to effectively combine various units into a single army without relying on payment by the state. Instead, Rome seems to have relied upon a sense of obligation (civic duty for her citizens and treaties for her allies), along with the promise of booty after the war which included both the usual forms of portable wealth (gold, silver, arms, armour, etc.) and increasingly land (although this was reserved for her own citizens during this period). But this system allowed Rome to have an almost endless supply of soldiers for her armies, which was not limited by troop type, organization, tactics or formation, or even state finances. The strength of the system was not in its inherent tactics, formations or equipment, but actually the absence of these things. The Roman military system, like Roman society at this time, was all about integration and incorporation.

The War Against Pyrrhus

Rome's expanded (and expanding) army was very quickly put to the test against one of the very best armies that the Mediterranean world had to offer in the early third century BC: that of Pyrrhus, king of Epirus, who came across to Italy at the request of the Greeks living in southern Italy. By the late fourth century BC, Rome was increasingly making her presence felt in southern Italy, having gobbled up the Greek communities in Campania, and started venturing into territory which had previously been controlled by the Greek *poleis* further south – causing regional tensions to rise. Although the Romans seem to have adopted a reasonably tempered approach to the Greeks as a whole, rarely attacking them directly and never without being provoked or at least a nominal invitation by an ally, it is clear that the Greeks had started to see the writing on the wall. Rome was coming. This led to Rome suddenly appearing more prominently in Greek histories and literature, as Greeks across the Mediterranean (but particularly in southern Italy) began to wonder about this new and emerging power, and an increased interest on the part of Greek *poleis* in Roman military actions as they worryingly watched the tide of Roman expansion creep ever closer to their doors.

The situation came to a head at the Greek community of Tarentum, near the heel of Italy. Tarentum initially came into conflict with Rome during the Second Samnite War, as she felt Rome was moving too far into her traditional sphere of interest and was increasingly in a position where she felt she must either 'push back or be pushed out'. However, as the people of Tarentum did not really want to try their luck against Rome's armies on their own, they asked their traditional ally Sparta for help. So in 303 BC, King Cleomenes of Sparta arrived in southern Italy with an army of 5,000 mercenaries (which was bolstered with 22,000 from Tarentum and her allies) to fight against Rome. Despite the fact that the Romans had just defeated the Samnites and had a powerful and seasoned army in the field, the unified Greek army was initially very successful and Cleomenes was able to win a number of battles and unify much of Magna Graecia under his banner. The Greeks were ultimately stopped by the Romans, but Tarentum seems to have been reasonably successful in her goals as she was able to sign a treaty with Rome in 302 BC which recognized the city's power in southern Italy, particularly in the Gulf of Tarentum. This was never going to be the end of the conflict, however. Roman expansion seems to have reached a critical mass and become a chain reaction which was almost impossible to contain, while on the other hand the entire Greek world was increasingly caught up in the Wars of the Successors following the death of Alexander the Great and the dissolution of his empire, resulting in a large number of powerful, ambitious and expansionist kingdoms looking for easy targets.

The next major development occurred in 282 BC, when a small Roman fleet arrived at Tarentum. Although the fleet was supposedly forced to land at Tarentum because of weather, the people of Tarentum seem to have seen this as a breach of the treaty of 302 BC and attacked the fleet, killing the Roman commander and sinking a number of the ships as they sat in the harbour. They then attacked the nearby community of Thurii, an ally of Rome, which they blamed for Rome's presence in the region, and readied for war. From the outset, the Tarentines knew they could not defeat Rome on their own, so they once again went to Sparta for help. However, this time Sparta had her own troubles to deal with and so the Tarentines had to look further afield for allies – ultimately recruiting the brilliant King Pyrrhus of Epirus. From the Tarentine point of view, this was something of a coup, as Pyrrhus was a renowned commander and a reasonably major figure in the Wars of the Successors, whose army represented one of the best the Mediterranean had to offer at the time – including both a sarissa-armed phalanx and elephants. For Pyrrhus, the invitation of Tarentum to come to Italy was also quite appealing. By 282 BC, Pyrrhus had lost most of his power in Greece to Lysimachus and was looking for a new region to focus on (and perhaps easier opponents to face than the great Hellenistic armies of the east) to try and carve out his own empire. The Tarentines also came offering an army of 350,000 local infantry and 20,000 cavalry (very little of which ever actually materialized) to bolster his forces once he arrived, making the deal almost irresistible. So in 281 BC, Pyrrhus crossed the Adriatic with an army of 3,000 cavalry, 20,000 infantry, 2,000 archers, 500 slingers and twenty elephants – a very formidable force (despite losing a number of elephants in the stormy crossing).

Pyrrhus went on to fight two major battles against the Romans, at Heracleia in 280 BC and Asculum in 279 BC, and technically won both – inflicting heavy casualties on the Romans and controlling the field of battle afterwards – although they famously came at a heavy cost, resulting in the phrase a 'Pyrrhic victory'. Indeed, after the Battle of Asculum Pyrrhus supposedly noted that 'if we are victorious in one more battle against the Romans, we shall be utterly ruined.'[9] The problem which Pyrrhus seems to have faced is that while the Romans were able to feed more and more soldiers, both allied and Roman, into their manipular structure, most of the losses that Pyrrhus took were irreplaceable. Like the army of Alexander the Great, the army of Pyrrhus featured a number of distinct and highly specialized units (the sarissa-armed phalanges which represented the core of his arm, the heavy cavalry which was his strike force, elephants as a terror weapon, light infantry to connect and screen the various other units, etc.) and in order to function effectively each unit needed to perform its duty. If any particular unit or facet of the army suffered heavy casualties, then the entire system broke down. Unfortunately for Pyrrhus, while active in Italy he was not able to replace any of the losses to his specialist units and was forced to simply reinforce his army with local forces from Tarrentum and her allies, including some of the Samnite tribes. Conversely, the manipular system of the Romans allowed them to field an army composed of any number of units from Roman, Latin and other allied areas, as most of them looked and fought in roughly the same manner, featuring the increasingly common Italic combination of an oblong shield and javelins.

Following the Battle of Asculum, Pyrrhus appears to have lost interest in Italy and crossed to Sicily to get involved in the ongoing conflict there. This seems to reflect something of a character flaw in Pyrrhus in that, although he was a brilliant tactician and was recognized as one of the best commanders in the field in all of antiquity (famously, Hannibal Barca noted that Pyrrhus ranked just behind Alexander the Great in this respect), he lacked the single-minded focus and strategic foresight to convert his victories on the battlefield into winning a war. Indeed, Antigonas Gonatas, one of Pyrrhus' contemporaries and rivals, once noted that Pyrrhus was 'very much like a player throwing dice that was able to make many fine throws but never understood how to use them when they were made'.[10] So in 278 BC, despite defeating the Romans in two successive battles, Pyrrhus left Italy for Sicily at the request of Syracuse to help them against the Carthaginians. Pyrrhus was active in Sicily for three years, leaving the Greeks of southern Italy to continue the war against Rome on their own, and only returned in 275 BC having become bored (and probably having worn out his welcome) in Sicily. In his absence, the Romans had been able to put together a string of victories against the Terrentines and, when he arrived, Pyrrhus and his forces found themselves engaged in a last-ditch effort to hold back the Roman tide. Pyrrhus' final battle against the Romans was at Beneventum, where the Romans were finally able to defeat him and his Greek and Samnite allies, forcing him to leave Italy permanently. The reasons for this victory are a bit hazy, although it most likely had something to do with the Romans finally finding a way to combat Pyrrhus' elephants (something which they may have figured out at Asculum), his losses over the past four years of war and probably some fatigue on the part of his army (as Pyrrhus had supposedly attempted a night march/assault on the Roman camp). The end result, however, was Rome's complete domination of southern Italy and a famous and resounding victory over one of the great armies, and great generals, of the Hellenistic world.

This seems to have been the moment when all in the Mediterranean turned their heads towards Italy and took notice of the new power in the region. Although Rome had been a budding power for almost a century before, the victory over the army of Pyrrhus (even if weakened by years of warfare) demonstrated that the Romans were more than just a regional force. Up to this point, the great Hellenistic kings and armies of the Mediterranean had only really had to worry about each other. Other local powers had occasionally presented some resistance, most notably the Carthaginians in Sicily, but for over fifty years the only significant defeats of Hellenistic kings and armies had come at the hands of other Hellenistic kings and armies. Rome's victory at Benventum in 275 BC changed that, and marked the beginning of the end for the Hellenistic way of war. Although the Hellenistic kingdoms would continue to fight and squabble over boundaries, from 275 BC onward there was a gradual swing in the balance of power in the Mediterranean from the east to the west.

Carthage

In the western Mediterranean, the other player was the great maritime power of Carthage. Founded by Phoenician sailors in the ninth century BC, as part of a wave of migration and colonization which started in the Levant and moved west, Carthage slowly emerged as one of the most important powers in the west by virtue of its territorial empire in North Africa, its trading network and an increasingly powerful navy. From the sixth century BC onward, the city represented one of the most powerful states in the western Mediterranean, jockeying for power and control of trade with the Greek communities of Sicily and Magna Graecia, and regularly venturing further north in Italy in search of both resources and trading partners. Rome's relationship with Carthage therefore went back centuries. Archaeology suggests that Punic merchants were active along the Tyrrhenian coast back in the Orientalising period and the Romans are recorded as signing a treaty with Carthage, which outlined zones of control and limited naval activity, back 'in the first year of the Republic' (although what this means and the exact date of the treaty have long been debated). The initial treaty between Carthage and Rome was followed up by two more in the fourth and third centuries BC which further defined the relationship, although overall things seem to have been generally amicable during this period as the interests of the two polities appear to have been confined to entirely different zones. Carthage, based in North Africa (modern day Tunisia), was predominantly a maritime power. With a massive trading network stretching across the Mediterranean, it was happy to leave Central and even Southern Italy to Rome so long as her ships remained unmolested, the markets stayed open and her influence in Sicily remained secure. From Rome's perspective, there was little reason to get into conflict with Carthage either. Although Rome was increasingly beginning to dabble in naval technology and maritime affairs, this was still, predominantly, a private enterprise. By the late fourth century BC, there seems to have been a move to secure the coast of Italy using military outposts (*coloniae maritimae*) and the creation of two small fleets in 311 BC led by *duovir navalis*, but for the most part Rome's interests were land-based at this time. Carthage and her naval empire were safe.

The expansion of Rome's empire into Southern Italy, however, and her conquest and integration of the Greek *poleis* of Magna Graecia changed the dynamic. When Rome conquered and integrated communities such as Neapolis, Capua and eventually Tarrentum, she also took on some of their interests – and these interests put the city into direct conflict with Carthage. The Greeks of Southern Italy and Sicily had been engaged in a long and sometimes violent struggle with Carthage over control of trade and harbours in the west. As a result, both Carthage and the various Greek communities had built huge navies to protect and extend their interests at sea and often fought major battles and minor engagements in and around the island of Sicily, whose key position in the Mediterranean allowed anyone who controlled it to control the trade around and across it. Previously, Rome's interests (as indicated by the early treaties) seem to have been generally concerned with securing her position in Central Italy. But with Rome's victory over Pyrrhus, and her incorporation of the Greek communities of Southern Italy, her interests expanded and seem to have increasingly aligned with her new Greek allies toward control of Sicily. This did not happen immediately it seems, as Sicilian historian Philinus reported that the final treaty between Rome and Carthage, dated to 279/8 BC, once again reaffirmed Carthaginian control of Sicily. However, by the mid-260s BC, Rome had thought better of the matter.

In 264 BC, Rome was yet again (nominally at least) drawn into conflict with a great Mediterranean power by the entreaties of a weaker entity – in this instance, by the Mamertines of Messina who lobbied for help against the tyrant Hiero II of Syracuse – although it is likely, as with the war against the Samnites, that Rome was not an entirely unwilling participant. Quite the opposite in fact as, even if the account of Philinus regarding the treaty of 279/8 BC is to be ignored and the Romans had not recognized Carthaginian control of Sicily in the 270s BC (and there is sustained scholarly debate on this issue), the Romans would have known, based on over 200 years of treaties and a longstanding relationship, that any activity on the island would likely be taken as an overt act of aggression against Carthaginian interests. Crossing the Straights of Messenia might not necessarily mean war, but it was not an act which would be taken lightly. When Rome joined the side of the Mamertines against Syracuse, Hiero turned immediately to the other great regional power – Carthage – for help. Given Carthage's foothold and long-standing involvement in the area, not to mention her overwhelming naval advantage, it is probable that Hiero thought he had enlisted a 'ringer' – although the long-term implications of this involvement may have been worrying as it is likely that Carthage would have claimed all of the spoils of war (including territory) for herself.

In the end, however, Hiero and Syracuse did not have to worry about Carthage's increased influence or claim on Sicily as the Romans were able to win a comprehensive victory, despite the initial Carthaginian advantage at sea. The war itself went back and forth over its twenty-three-year run (264–241 BC), but the Romans were largely the aggressors throughout. In 261 BC, Rome won the Battle of Agrigentum in southern Sicily, which represented the first major engagement and one of the only significant land battles fought. This was followed by a Carthaginian victory at sea in 260 BC at the Lipari Islands. After this defeat the Romans quickly bolstered their fleet and added some interesting pieces of equipment – most notably the famous *corvus*, or boarding bridge, which allowed them to engage and board enemy ships far more efficiently – which may have led to the subsequent naval victory at Mylae. However, following this loss at sea the Carthaginians were able to win back some territory in 260 and 259 BC, only to lose it again the next year. In the early 250s BC, the Romans attempted an invasion of Africa, which was thwarted by the loss at Cape Ecnomus in 256 BC, although the Romans continued to engage the Carthaginians on their home soil through the general Regulus and his army until he was eventually defeated by the Spartan mercenary Xanthippus, who had taken service in Carthage. Things swung back and forth, and indeed the Carthaginians were able to win some significant gains on Sicily, until 241 BC and the Battle of the Aegates Islands where a Roman fleet was finally able to comprehensively defeat the vast majority of the remaining Carthaginian fleet, effectively ending the war.

Rome's conflict with Carthage obviously continued and Rome went on to fight her greatest war against the Carthaginians in the final years of the third century BC – the Second Punic War, against Hannibal Barca (a war which is, unfortunately, beyond the scope of this volume). But despite the fact that her most significant conflicts were arguably yet to come, the Roman approach and attitude toward Carthage, and possibly the wider Mediterranean world, seems to have been firmly established by this point. The transition from Rome's early treaties with Carthage (and possibly as late as the 270s BC), where the Romans seem to have been largely concerned with securing their position in Italy, to Rome's aggressive expansion into Sicily, nominally at the request of a minor power but clearly pushing her own agenda in the region, shows a dramatic shift in attitude. Rome was no longer content to sit on the sidelines. Filled with confidence after the victory over Pyrrhus and backed by a large, ever-increasing collection of allies (mobilized and unified via the manipular army), Rome increasingly pushed her interests further and further afield.

Rome's Concept of Empire

The late fourth and third centuries BC witnessed the real birth of empire in Rome. While the second century BC saw the most significant expansion of Rome's foreign territories – with the conquest of Spain along with parts of the eastern and southern Mediterranean – all of this merely represented the expansion of a system created during the preceding period. Rome laid down the basic principles of her empire with her expansion beyond the close confines of Central Italy and measures like the creation of her first province (Sicily) and the development and delineation of powers such as *imperium*. Fundamental to this was the creation of a 'philosophy of empire', or approach to conquered lands and peoples, which set out the principles which governed Roman interactions with these entities.

A huge amount has been written on this topic and, while some broad areas of agreement have emerged, a detailed model – particularly for the third century BC – has yet to be established. One of the reasons behind this continued debate is the perceived lack of a consistent attitude or approach displayed by Rome's assemblies or the Senate in foreign policy and relations. In interactions with various communities and kingdoms, even as late as the mid-second century BC, Rome's actions and reactions are often seen as erratic and inconsistent, which arguably reflects the highly personal nature of Roman politics. Each situation seems to have been dealt with in an *ad hoc* manner as it arose, and although the Roman penchant for precedent was always present, the immediate needs and desires of the Roman Senate (and those individuals who happened to hold sway in the Senate at a given time) seem to have been given priority. This means that Roman foreign policy is often seen as an extension of domestic policy and the personal competition which defined the Roman elite. While this is clearly true, at least to a certain extent, there are still broad principles which generally governed these interactions.

One of the most important principles, and one which was often ignored by scholars in the nineteenth and early twentieth centuries (writing in an age of nationalist empires), is that in the early third century BC, Roman identity and *Romanitas* were still reasonably new things – that Rome, as a state and the head of an empire, was still figuring out her own identity at the same time as she was imposing her political will on others. Although Rome's victory over the Latins in 338 BC clearly indicates a *terminus ante quem* for the creation of a distinct Roman political identity – a mid-fourth century BC date which is actually indirectly supported by Gelzer and more recently Hölkeskamp's arguments concerning the origins of a distinctly Roman elite – this means that when Rome began to put together the first major pieces of her empire in the early third century BC this identity was only a generation or so old.[11] While in some cases, for instance in the creation of modern nation-states, this recent birth could have resulted in a more fervent or defensive attitude towards it, in the case of Rome it seems to have led to the opposite. While Rome's elites, and their fortunes and futures, were permanently linked to the community by this point, Roman citizenship had yet to develop into a sought-after commodity and Roman politics – even the uppermost levels – were relatively open. The ending of the Struggle of the Orders in the final years of the fourth century BC had finally and permanently mixed the heterogeneous plebeians and the gentilicial patricians in almost every facet of Roman politics and society. The result of this was a new Roman citizen body, but one which was still finding its feet. When it came to foreign policy then, although the Romans clearly did have a sense of 'us' and 'them' – particularly when it came to truly foreign peoples – this was not as pronounced as often thought. Roman society and Roman politics were therefore relatively open during this period, and capable of true integration – something reflected in the Roman approach to things such as citizenship, the position of manumitted slaves, etc. – although whether the foreign peoples were themselves open to this integration is another matter entirely.

A second key principle to understanding Rome's approach to empire was that it was based on a centuries-old approach to warfare embodied by the archaic grant of *imperium* which, as argued previously, seems to have represented a contract between the community and a warlord/clan leader whereby the community bound itself to the clan and clan leader, possibly in the form of *clientes*, in exchange for protection. This relationship, and *imperium* itself, naturally developed in significant ways as both the community and the warlords/clan leaders evolved during the course of the fifth and fourth centuries BC, but some of the basic principles remained intact. One of the most fundamental of these was the strictly extramural and highly individual nature of the power which a Roman general wielded, whereby – although imbued with power by the civic authority – he acted and commanded based on his own right and auspices. As a result, the degree to which Roman generals in the field should be viewed as representatives of Rome must be weighed against how much they still existed as independent warlords – a tension which seems to have existed throughout the Republican period. Roman generals were clearly understood to have responsibilities and obligations to both the community and their soldiers, but these should be understood as existing in the same sphere as those between a patron and a client – and were therefore flexible and open to interpretation.

Conclusion

The 100-year period from 350 to 250 BC represents a period of massive change in Roman society, as it saw Rome evolve from a single city-state in Central Italy to master of a substantial territorial empire encompassing all of Italy and Sicily and saw her ascension to the single most dominant entity in the western Mediterranean. But despite the creation of an empire, Rome and her generals were still a product of their development and the city's approach to her newly-won territory reflected this. Rome did not suddenly learn how to govern her captured lands and peoples or change her personality or character overnight. Instead, the Romans continued to approach matters largely as they had before, allowing individual elites to dictate war and foreign policy as suited their needs (albeit with the rest of Rome's elite taking a keen interest, lest their own interests be affected) and with Rome's armies acting as the mechanism to accomplish this, albeit in an increasingly regularized fashion. This is why Rome's approach to empire in the third century, and even the second century BC, seems so haphazard. There was no single Roman foreign policy or grand strategic plan. Rome's elites continued to function much as they had before, using warfare as a means for personal and family competition, largely irrespective of the benefit to the state or community. Indeed, what benefits there were, were often incidental during this period, and it was only with the campaigns of the second century BC – after the great watershed moment of the Second Punic War – that Rome's armies and Roman foreign policy began to reflect the will of a coherent and cohesive state. Although, as anyone familiar with the events of the first century BC will know, things would very soon revert back to this more archaic *modus operandi*.

Conclusions

The development of Rome's early armies and early Roman warfare have always been thought to mirror the development of early Rome itself. Roman historians such as Livy presented Rome as largely eternal and unchanging – at least at its core. The outward trappings changed, the city grew and transitioned from one made of brick to one of marble, and the appearance of Rome's armies changed, from Romulus' ragtag tribal army to the victorious legions of Augustus, but what it meant to be Roman never changed. And indeed, this was the point of Livy's work and why he chose to write about early Rome in the first place – by explaining what it meant to be a 'good Roman' in the past, he could provide examples (*exempla*) which Romans in his own day could follow. Livy, and the rest of Rome's historians, needed to make the early city relevant to their contemporary population in order for their works to be effective – and the way they did this was by suggesting that the core attributes of Rome, including the principles underpinning her army, had changed minimally if at all.

This is not to say that *nothing* changed, however. Despite the limited and cryptic evidence which Rome's early historians had to work with when trying to piece together the early history of the city, there were clearly a number of dramatic changes which did occur, which were recorded and needed to be explained – the transition from a monarchy to a Republic, Rome's various constitutional reforms in the mid-fifth and mid-fourth centuries BC, Rome's various military developments, etc. But despite their superficial impact, the society which witnessed these developments was always framed in a way where it seems to have remained largely unchanged throughout. The aristocracy before and after 509 BC was described as being largely the same, as was the plebeian population, and indeed both bear a striking resemblance to the same groups as they appeared in late Republican society. Similarly, the army, although it regularly changed its equipment, tactics and formation during the Archaic period, maintained a shockingly similar makeup and character in the narrative – which also (suspiciously) mirrors what one would expect from a late Republican army. So was Livy right? Did Rome really remain largely unchanged, at least socially and culturally, for all of those years? As you will have learned from the preceding chapters, the answer is 'probably not'.

Reading outside of Livy's (and his colleagues') explicit narrative of consistency, there is strong evidence for quite a bit of change in Roman society during the period from *c.* 753 BC to *c.* 250 BC – and indeed, common sense should suggest this. No society remains static for over 500 years, and particularly not one which came into contact with so many different cultures on such a regular basis. Perhaps the biggest difference which emerges from exploring this 'alternate' history of early Rome is that the social and civic cohesion which Roman historians suggested was present from the city's very foundation actually took quite a while to develop, and that the various struggles which Rome witnessed – between the aristocracy and the *rex*, between the patricians and the plebeians, etc. – were not necessarily internal struggles for power, but growing pains caused by the incorporation of new groups.

Roman society, far from being static and eternal, was actually constantly growing and developing. The image which emerges from a more detailed study of the evidence can be interpreted as a community slowly bringing the region's powerful, warlike, rural clans together around an urban hub during the seventh, sixth and fifth centuries BC, with the resulting *res publica* representing a flexible power-sharing arrangement between the various groups. The process was long and messy, and it is highly unlikely that any of the early systems or institutions had anything resembling the complexity of Rome's later magistracies and laws. Instead, Rome's monarchy – and later the Republic – seem to have relied upon existing standards which did not require a strong state backing (family laws and the power of the *paterfamilias*, religious laws, economic norms, etc.) as the basis for their government and society. However, Livy was not wholly wrong in arguing for consistency. Some of the main characters in his narrative – particularly the powerful clans or *gentes* and Rome's urban population – do seem to have existed throughout, although their role, relationship and arguably aspects of their character obviously changed.

Mapping this revised version of early Roman society back onto the development of warfare and the Roman army, the end result is a slightly different picture from that explicitly presented in the literary sources. Although the basic battle narratives arguably remain intact (if these can be believed at all for the early period), the military structures, aims and motivations for warfare all appear to have changed. Most notably, the resultant model is one where Roman warfare during the Regal period and first century of so of the Republic, even that conducted by magistrates like the *rex* and the archaic consuls, actually seems to represent clan-based warfare (and indeed where the Roman army can be considered a gentilicial or clan-based army for all intents and purposes) until it is gradually replaced by ever more civic and community-based forces during the fifth and fourth centuries BC. These armies were organized and mobilized by powerful clan leaders, either occupying an official position within the city as a *rex* or consul, or not – as there are countless references in the sources to private warfare conducted by clans. The armies, both nominally 'Roman' or private, seem to have pursued the same objectives – largely raiding for portable wealth – and their victories (and indeed their losses) generally had little impact on the community as a whole. It was only in the second half of the fifth century BC that Rome's armies began to separate themselves from their strictly gentilicial or clan-based counterparts. Likely linked to a range of different factors, including the increase in agriculture and the desire for land as a spoil of war, the rise of non-gentilicial nobles in the city, the increasingly settled nature of the clans around the city and their strengthening attachments to the city, etc., Rome experimented with a number of different innovations which served to make warfare more communal. This included the creation of the consular tribunes and likely a tinkering with the archaic power of *imperium* (itself probably based on the awesome power of the *paterfamilias*), although all of these seem to have failed – more than likely stymied by the egos of clans – until the entire city was brought to its knees by the Gallic sack *c.* 390 BC.

The Rome which emerged from the Gallic sack seems to have been a rather different city from that which existed before it. While previously Rome's elites had been happy to continue the old ways of doing things and prefered engaging in individual and clan-based warfare, the sack by the Gauls had demonstrated the weakness of disunity. Following the sack, Rome quickly reverted full-time to the consular tribunes as military leaders and scrambled to secure her position and expand her military base. The city quickly created new tribes out of the territory captured from Veii a few years previously and started to create citizen colonies, or *municipia* as at Tusculum, which were liable for military service, along with new alliances with her neighbours. All of this suggests a new defensive imperative in Rome which resulted in a throwing out of the old, aristocratic mode of warfare and raiding which had lingered on to the end of the fifth century BC and the full-time adoption of a more unified approach. All of this was evidently reactionary though, and did not seem to represent a perfect or indeed well thought-out system, as Rome's continued experiments indicate. A few decades later, Rome once again tinkered with her military command structure. This moment, in the 370s and 360s BC, represents the real introduction of a coherent military system for the community, marked by Rome's reintroduction of a revised form of the consulship and the construction of her great city walls. The city walls clearly delineated 'us' and 'them' in (literally) concrete terms, while the reinvented consulship seems to have represented the true precursor to the middle and late Republican office. Rome also began to expand territorially during this period. In previous years, Rome had acquired territory in a limited and generally piecemeal fashion, and usually only when portable booty was unavailable. In the fourth century BC, Rome gradually expanded her territorial holdings, and particularly *ager Romanus* (land held communally by the Roman state) – a process which picked up steam as Rome neared the end of the fourth century and entered the third century BC.

As noted previously, much of this interpretation flies in the face of the standard view of early Roman warfare and society. This model suggests that Rome's early armies were not really 'Roman' in the same way as later forces, as they effectively functioned as extensions of aristocratic clans, and hints at a fragmented society which was driven together (at least in part) by fear and desperation in the fourth century BC. Additionally, this reinterpretation casts doubt on the traditional sequence for Roman political development. The army was traditionally seen as the voice and embodiment of the state, most notably through the Centuriate Assembly, which should mean that any warfare performed by the army was, by definition, an act of the state. Indeed, how Rome's political system and its development are mapped on to this military model still represents a major issue. By far the easiest approach has been simply to move the development of Rome's various institutions later in the Republic – and many scholars have done just that. Although the literary sources ascribe the creation of the Centuriate Assembly to the Regal period and the reign of Servius Tullius, the account is so full of anachronisms that it is clear that at least some aspects represent later additions. Taking the mid-fifth century BC as the starting point for this assembly does make some sense, as associating the creation of economic classes with the creation of the censorship is logical, as is its association with a new form of military leadership in the consular tribunes. Additionally, it is clear from a number of laws (most notably the *lex Papiria Julia* of 430 BC) that Rome was increasingly shifting over to an economy based on bronze currency, hinting that this is an appropriate time to suggest the beginning of this type of economic differentiation. But although this reinterpretation makes logical sense, it relies more on deduction and logic than solid evidence, and is therefore open to critiques of circularity and bias.

The end result of all of this is that the Roman army which marched into the late fourth and early third centuries BC – which defeated the Samnites, Pyrrhus and eventually the Carthaginians – was most likely a slightly different entity than previously thought. It suggests that the existence of a Roman army which regularly acted in the interests of the community as a whole was a relatively new phenomenon in this period. But with the acquisition of more and more *ager Romanus* in the late fourth and early third centuries BC, increased strategic conquests and the creation of new alliance networks, by the end of the fourth century BC Roman warfare had changed its goals dramatically from the old days of raiding for portable wealth. Indeed, with the reinvention of the consulship in 376/367 BC and the eventual ending of the Struggle of the Orders, both Rome's army and her political system finally reflected the unity which Livy and Rome's other historians wanted to see far earlier. However, this youth was not a detriment, but rather an advantage. Although Rome's army was not in fact the well-honed and long-established fighting machine which had learned from various enemies (including the Etruscans, Gauls, Greeks and Samnites), but instead a new creation, formed from the remnants of Rome's aristocratic, clan-based warbands which had only recently fully unified in the face of a Gallic threat, this meant it was also adaptive. The fact that Rome's army was so young, and was formed from uniting the previously disparate elements of the city, is probably why it was able to integrate new units and peoples so effectively during this period. The manipular system, rather than representing a broken-up phalanx, instead may have represented an increasingly formalized and cohesive collection of clans and other military groups. So, although Rome's army *c.* 300 BC was arguably still struggling to find its identity, as was the city it emerged from, both had settled on a defining theme – strength through integration and expansion.

Notes

Introduction

1. Livy 6.1.
2. Those historians who specialize or focus on other periods often take the privilege of adopting rather 'simplistic' approaches to the record for early Rome – usually taking the extant sources at their word.
3. There are, obviously, exceptions to this – most notably the study of laws and particular social, religious or political reforms where a record may have been preserved.

Chapter 1

1. There is some debate on this issue, as writers like Licinius Macer claim to have found new annals, most notably the *libri lintei* or linen books, although many scholars now think these were invented to give his account (and the elaborations contained therein) a bit more credence.
2. Dionysius of Halicarnassus' work, *Roman Antiquities*, could also be included here although it is technically not part of the annalistic movement.
3. Dion. Hal. *Ant. Rom.* 2.7 (Trans. Cary)
4. Var. *LL.* 5.89.1
5. Plut. *Rom.* 13.1
6. Dion. Hal. *Ant. Rom.* 2.16 (Trans. Cary)
7. Dion. Hal. *Ant Rom.* 4.19 (Trans Cary).
8. Gellius *NA* 6.13
9. *Ineditum Vaticanum* 3 (Trans Cornell).
10. Gellius *NA* 6.13. (Trans. Sage).
11. Festus 100L. (Trans Sage). The slight difference in amounts between the accounts, and interestingly neither one matching up with the numbers given by Livy and Dionysius (both 100,000 assess), likely represents different historical traditions or perhaps a later figure after the bronze ass was devalued in 141 BC.
12. Dion. Hal. Ant. Rom. 11. 23. (Trans Cary).
13. Dion. Hal. Ant. Rom. 16.3. (Trans Cary).
14. Livy 1.24.1-3 (Trans. Foster)
15. Livy 1.10.4 (Trans. Foster)
16. Livy 2.6.7–10 (Trans. Foster)
17. Oakley (1985), pp. 392–410.
18. For further material on this subject see Bispham in Bradley's excellent *Greek and Roman Colonization. Origins, Ideologies and Interactions* (2006).
19. Bietti Sestieri (1992) 200, 208.

Chapter 2

1. Cicero. *Top.* 29 (trans. Smith).
2. Bietti Sestieri (1992).

3. Dion. Hal. *Ant Rom.* 2.2.1–3 (Trans. Cary).
4. Livy. 1.8.5–6 (Trans. Foster).
5. Momigliano (1963): 112.
6. Taylor (1960): 35.
7. Tablet of Lyon, 2 (Trans. Smallwood).
8. Livy 2.48.5-10. (Trans Foster).
9. Livy 3.15.5–6. (Trans. Foster).
10. Livy 2.40.
11. Livy 5.16.4–6. (Trans. Foster).
12. Bietti Sestieri (1992): 244–253.

Chapter 3
1. Polyb. 6.18 (trans. Paton).
2. Alföldi 1965: 72–84; Howarth 1997: 71.
3. Livy 4.17–33.

Chapter 4
1. The two dates given for this event are 390 BC, in the Varronian chronology, and 387 BC.
2. Livy 6.1.
3. Scholars have searched for a 'burn layer' associated with the early fourth century BC for years and while, particularly in recent years, a range of possible indicators for this have been unearthed the evidence is far from conclusive.
4. Plut. *Cam.* 22.
5. Livy 7.1.10.
6. Plut. *Cam.* 1.32–33.
7. Dumézil (1980).
8. Gelzer (1969).
9. Cicero *Ad Fam* 1.9.25 (Trans. Shuckburgh).
10. Quesada Sanz (2006) 252.
11. Livy 6.32 (Trans. Foster)
12. Cornell (1990) 367.
13. Salmon (1969) 40–45.

Chapter 6
1. Harris (1979) and Rosenstein (1990).
2. See particularly Keegan (1994) for discussion.
3. It is worth noting that although the sources, and many modern scholars, refer to the Samnites as a single, monolithic entity, they most likely represented – at best – a loose federation of tribes who joined forces when it suited them.
4. This refers to the introduction of the *stipendium*, associated with the siege of Veii c. 400 BC.
5. Livy 8.8.3–14 (Trans. Foster).
6. *Ineditum Vaticanum* 3 (Trans. Cornell).
7. Van Wees (2004).
8. See Chagnon (1997) for discussion.
9. Plut. *Pyrr.* 21 (Trans. Perrin).
10. Plut. *Pyrr.* 26 (Trans. Perrin).
11. Gelzer (1969) and Hölkeskamp (1987).

Bibliography

Alföldi, A. (1965) *Early Rome and the Latins*. University of Michigan Press, Ann Arbor.

Bietti Sestieri, A.M. (1992) The Iron Age Community of Osteria Dell'Osa : A Study of Socio-Political Development in Central Tyrrhenian Italy. *New Studies in Archaeology*. Cambridge University Press, Cambridge.

Bradley, G.J., Wilson, J.P. & Bispham, E. (2006) *Greek and Roman Colonization : Origins, Ideologies and Interactions*. Classical Press of Wales, Swansea.

Chagnon, N. (1997) *Yanomamo*. Harcourt Brace College Publishers, Fort Worth.

Cornell, T. (1990) The Recovery of Rome. In: F.W. Walbank, A.E. Astin, M.W. Frederiksen & R.M.Ogilvie (eds), *The Cambridge Ancient History Volume 7, Part 2: The Rise of Rome to 220 BC, Second edition*. Cambridge University Press, Cambridge.

Dumézil, G. (1980) *Camillus: A Study of Indo-European Religion as Roman History*. University of California Press, Berkeley.

Gelzer, M. (1969) *The Roman Nobility (trans. Robin Seager)*. Oxford University Press, Oxford.

Harris, W.V. (1979) *War and Imperialism in Republican Rome*. Oxford University Press, Oxford.

Hölkeskamp, K.-J. (1987) *Die Entstehung der Nobilität: Studien zur sozialen und politischen Geschichte der Römischen Republik im 4. Jhdt. V. Chr.* F. Steiner Verlag, Stuttgart.

Howarth, R.S. (1997) Rome and the Latins: A New Model. Unpublished PhD thesis, Department of History, The University of Illinois at Urbana-Champaign, Champaign.

Keegan, J. (1994) *A History of Warfare*. Pimlico, London.

Oakley, S.P. (1985) Single Combat in the Roman Republic. *Classical Quarterly*, 35: 392–410.

Quesada Sanz, F. (2006) Not So Different: Individual Fighting Techniques and Small Unit Tactics of Roman and Iberian Armies within the Framework of Warfare in the Hellenistic Age. *Pallas*, 70: 245–63.

Rosenstein, N. (1990) Imperatores Victi*: Military Defeat and Aristocratic Competition in the Middle and Late Republic*. University of California Press, Berkeley.

Salmon, E.T. (1969) *Roman Colonization under the Republic*. Thames & Hudson, London.

Taylor, L.R. (1960) *The Voting Districts of the Roman Republic: The Thirty-Five Urban and Rural Tribes*, Papers and Monographs of the American Academy in Rome, Vol. 20. Rome.

Wees, H. van (2004) *Greek Warfare: Myths and Realities*. Duckworth, London.

Further Reading

Cornell, T. (1995) *The Beginnings of Rome: Italy and Rome from the Bronze Age to the Punic Wars (c. 1000–264 BC)*. Routledge, London.

Flower, H. (2010) *Roman Republics*. Princeton University Press, Princeton, NJ.

Forsythe, G. (2005) *A Critical History of Early Rome: From Prehistory to the First Punic War*. University of California Press, Berkeley.

Fulminante, F. (2014) *The Urbanisation of Rome and* Latium Vetus*: From the Bronze Age to the Archaic Era*. Cambridge University Press, Cambridge.

Harris, W.V. (1979) *War and Imperialism in Republican Rome*. Clarendon Press, Oxford.

Smith, C.J. (2006) *The Roman Clan: The* Gens *from Ancient Ideology to Modern Anthropology*. Cambridge University Press, Cambridge.

Wiseman, T.P. (1995) *Remus: A Roman Myth*. Cambridge University Press, Cambridge.

Index